# YOUR
# *Tapestry*
# FOR *Life*

by
*Carol Greenidge*

**EXCELL**
**PUBLISHING**

# *Dedication*

*This Book Is Dedicated to You*

This paperback edition published by:

Excell Publishing
P.O. Box 3472
Evergreen, Colorado 80439 USA

Library of Congress Catalog Card Number: 94-90687
ISBN: 0-9644235-0-2

First Edition: January 1995

# *Contents*

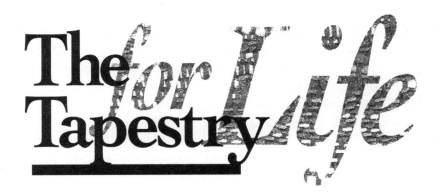

# The Tapestry for Life

**T**HE WEAVING OF the tapestry of your life exists within your mind and heart. You have the freedom and choice at every moment to be, do, and have all you desire. You possess the power and strength. The "pathway" is coded into the many words woven into these pages and various topics. Some of the principles are related to you consciously, while others are subtle and to be uncovered through your own unconscious process of bringing to the conscious mind universal truths along with your own personal truth.

How you integrate the contents of this book into your life is your decision. It may be useful to sit down and write out those inspirations that come to you at the end of each topic in order to find your own personal truth in the process of self-discovery. It is up to you to weave all the pieces together in order to understand the secrets of life. The intent of this book is to stimulate you to empower yourself to create your own unique tapestry and to remind you that you are in control of your life. You can change or alter the colors, design, and shape of your own personal tapestry of life through your thoughts, feelings, attitudes, beliefs, words, and actions. You have choice at every moment and the freedom to do so.

Time spent by yourself in silence each day will greatly assist you to center and focus on your truth. The listening at all times to your inner voice of guidance (or intuition) will assist you to thread your way to completion—free of struggle. Trust and allow life and others to be. You may be unable to see the perfection and beauty of your finished tapestry at this moment, but realize that the process is perfect for what you need to learn.

You have the opportunity to select the colors (or emotions) you desire. What will be the values and hues? Will your tapestry appear warm or cool, gentle or intense, subtle or vibrant, simple or complex, large or small? Will the fibers of your thoughts be thick or thin, dull or shiny, fine or coarse, smooth or rough, bright or subdued? Will your design of action be bold or weak, focused or scattered, flowing or interrupted, positive or negative? Is your creation in integrity with yourself and others? Will it be a tapestry that is responsible with appropriate commitment, trust, and belief in yourself?

What does your completed tapestry reveal and represent? Is it free of restrictions and limiting beliefs and doubts? Is it intertwined with a glorious array of brilliant color and interesting textures and shapes? How does it make you feel to examine it? Since it is incomplete at present, you can change the weaving process to create what you desire. If it is not exciting enough, enliven it. If it is too random, bring it under control. It belongs to you, and you are the creator at every moment.

You have the Life Force Energy of the Universe to assist you. Be still and listen. You have greater power than you imagine, and you can alter your finished life's tapestry. Ask for assistance from the Power Within and Without, and **IT IS YOURS**. You are not alone. The weaving requires attention to the outer visible side and also the unseen inner layer. The beautiful work of art that is **YOU** begins in your heart. Your finished, embellished, magnificent tapestry complete with threads of silver and gold unites soul, body, mind, and spirit.

Best wishes for your creation!

# Love for Life

**A**T PRESENT IN MOST societies the concept of love is typically linked with romance. This is true for many, but a far deeper, more powerful love overrides even the greatest heights of romantic passion. Many individuals are unaware of this higher form of love even though reference to it certainly has been made throughout recorded history. Each who discovers "pure love" has knowledge of a very different state of being because the experience is all encompassing. No one who has had his or her heart opened ever forgets the overwhelming feeling of warmth, security, and fulfillment emanating from the heart center to every cell of the body.

What creates this feeling which represents a deep sense of oneness with all that exists? This perception is accompanied by an even greater knowledge that all is perfect—even if the experience lasts only a brief period. Similar to an addiction, once people have experienced this "oneness" they may spend years attempting to duplicate it within the feeling sensations of the physical body which they feel symbolize the true essence of love.

Why does this wonderful feeling of love and oneness dissipate? The answer is simple. A negative thought, feeling, or emotion enters to dispel the bliss. Is there anything that you can do to maintain the ultimate experience of blissful love? Knowing your true nature assists you to live in the state of love at all times. Awareness of your true human nature may become lost as negativity creeps into your life. Every day there are countless choices to be made, and often love does not prevail over anger, fear, doubt, greed, or various other negative emotions. The truth is always present but unrealized due to a lack of conscious awareness. From this day forward, know that choice is always available to you. You can choose, with your mind and heart, any feeling or emotion you desire. You can even choose the way you want to think and the context of those thoughts. Then why do people live in fear, anger, and disillusionment? The reason is because awareness, trust, and belief have not been firmly established in their consciousness.

If you are reared in a household of angry, fearful, controlling people, this may be regarded as an ordinary state of existence. If your friends are jealous, suspicious, and resentful, this too may be considered status quo. A gradual disintegration has developed within the human essence which originally was conceived and born in love and bliss.

You begin now in your present circumstances and state of awareness. Allow no judgment as to where you are in consciousness or concerning those who collaborated to put you there. The past can be put to rest if you choose to allow it to be. What is of essence is how you view both your past and present states of mind and emotion. You could indulge yourself and spend many hours, or even a lifetime, demonstrating a "woe is me" attitude and undeniably receive support and sympathy from others who relate to what you are feeling. You could strike out in anger at the world due to the "bad hand" you feel fate has dealt you. **OR** you could make the choice to close the door on the negativity of the past, except to acknowledge what you have learned from it, and decide to enter the world of love, trust, and belief in the positive.

What you have believed or chosen in the past results in the various aspects of your life weaving together to create your present consciousness and life experiences. Choosing only the **POS-ITIVE** results in positive effects. Negativity need not exist in your life. When it does, you have made the conscious or unconscious decision to allow it in.

How do you recognize when you have opened the door to negativity? What are the early warning signs you can consciously notice? The most readily apparent way to know, even before your intellect can tell you, is through the sensations in your physical body. You will *not* feel the blissful, unified state of love described previously. You could experience a wide spectrum of emotions which permeate your very being. Fear, anger, resentment, hate, jealousy, and doubt can all be felt in the physical body as pain, stress, nervousness, anxiety, faintness, tightness, heaviness, headaches or queasiness in the stomach area. What you sense can essentially be described as a feeling of discomfort. Since unconscious events and relationships have the ability to trigger these sensations at any time, what can you do to dispel them in order to return to your original natural state of love? This may seem like a difficult challenge, but in actuality it is extremely simple. All you have to do is make the conscious decision to feel the way you want to feel. Following this, you disallow and reject any doubts that you are strong and powerful enough to achieve and maintain your desired state. You can do it, and each time you choose to reverse negative feelings and to believe and trust that you can maintain freewill positive choice, it will become easier.

Eventually you engage in a positive process like the following:

- You become aware of an unpleasant or uncomfortable sensation in your body.

- You acknowledge and accept it and know it is there as an aid to give you needed information.

- You identify or describe the sensation and may or may not know the cause. Some causes can be triggered in the subconscious mind.

❀ You remember you have freewill choice as to how you desire to feel.

❀ You make the choice. To grow and achieve greater happiness in life, it is recommended you choose to replace the negative (or uncomfortable emotion) with a positive one.

❀ You consciously state to yourself what it is you desire to feel, such as "I choose to feel happy (loving, generous, secure, forgiving)." The idea is to select the feeling exactly opposite to the negative emotion you previously experienced. "I choose love" always works.

❀ Imagine how the positive emotion feels.

❀ Allow yourself to move into this chosen positive state, deeply feel it, and trust and believe you can maintain it. The choice to do so is truly *yours*.

❀ Be grateful you have this ability.

By following the preceding process, you can dramatically change your present reality, and you can do so at any time in order to create a blissful, happy, secure feeling of love. This is a gift that has been given to you. The more you use it, the greater and faster the results will come—automatically—and eventually you can perform this process almost at the speed of light without having to methodically proceed step-by-step. You will be aware of discomfort (negativity) and instantly move into the positive.

What is the end result? You will feel the warm, happy, exhilarated sensations described most appropriately as love and bliss. From being able to create your desired state at this level, you will feel more powerful and confident that you can transfer these methods into all areas of your life for the purpose of taking control and being, doing, and having all you desire. The purpose of this book is to provide you with the tools. The "creation" is what you will discover as you and your life's tapestry unfold— exactly as you choose. You will be given the raw materials. The finished product is up to you. Constant monitoring of how you feel will be of great benefit as you become aware at every second that you can choose to change any sensations you desire.

There is a powerful benevolent force in the Universe that is always available to assist you to be aware and intuitively know your most appropriate choices. The voice of intuition is perpetually present within you. All you have to do is listen to it and then trust what information you receive. This power is constantly available to help you achieve your ideal state of being. When you follow its advice, you experience comfort, confidence, security, joy, and a loving, warm feeling. When you disregard this inner knowing, discomfort, unhappiness, frustration, fear, doubt, and regret can result.

The forces of the Universe work with you internally and externally at all times with love as the ultimate goal. Remember to remember. That is the key.

# Forgiveness for Life

**F**ORGIVENESS MAY APPEAR to be a strange topic in today's world in which man often feels he must struggle to survive and sometimes does so by trampling on others' free will. However, letting go is an essential basis behind the ability to move forward in life. The act of forgiveness begins when love enters in, and it is of course a freewill choice. Whoever chooses forgiveness is truly blessed because it is of great importance in everyone's evolution. Whenever you forgive, your body's energy field shifts to greater clarity. When, as an individual consciousness, you choose blame and resentment and hold on to past negativity, your energy field is dark and cloudy, and inspiration cannot break through. Forgiveness is one of the easiest aspects of life to master because it involves only you, yourself, making the decision.

It must be clarified that forgiveness need not be considered a sacred act but one merely of releasing energy that is harmful to the physical, emotional, mental, and spiritual bodies. Those who harbor resentment and blame block themselves from the true gifts of the Universe because enlightenment cannot enter a person who is blocked by negative energy. The low level energy surrounding one who is holding on to past grievances and negativity can prove to be very serious in consequence because harm can also occur to the physical body. Resentments result in energy constrictions which affect physical well-being by creating blockages. Whenever you feel physical pain or discomfort, ask yourself if there is something you need to discharge from your thoughts or feelings. The first thing that comes to mind is usually the aspect that needs your immediate attention.

What occurs if you reject or ignore this idea and process of forgiveness? Initially you may be able to continue in life perhaps feeling irritated or like you have a "chip" on your shoulder. Later on your disturbed mental state may develop into deep resentment, anger, frustration, hatred, or other intense negative emotions—even stress, anxiety, and depression. Eventually, undealt with, the end result can be physical illness or imbalance in your emotional being or both. Whatever the cause, the end result may be similar. How do you overcome this negative process and move instead toward wholeness, oneness, love, and letting go?

First you must have an understanding of your feelings and how they originated. As a young child you were extremely open and vulnerable to the influences of others. You most likely witnessed parents, teachers, siblings, friends, and relatives demonstrating a spirit of anger and resentment which could serve as an example from a role model. Only rarely was the concept of true forgiveness revealed to you by those who were highly aware. Why was this condition so prevalent? The energy of anger and frustration is highly "contagious." Superficially it may appear easier to lash out and blame others than to let go and allow people and situations to be as they are.

This is not reality, however. In the long run as well as short term, "letting go" is the easier alternative. The strangeness or foreignness of it is what holds people back. Whenever forgiveness is withheld, suffering in some form manifests. Concentrate for a moment on a pain you have felt or wrong you have experienced at some time in your life, and question whether or not you consciously considered forgiveness (or letting go) as one of your options. The average man's nature has demonstrated that the first impulse is typically anger, frustration, or aggressive behavior with a desire for revenge or "getting even." Sometimes a driving determination for vindication can dominate a person's entire lifetime. Retaliation and feuding have become a central theme in books and movies. Revenge is considered by many to be appropriate and just. Certain individuals believe that if they have been wronged by another, it is appropriate and "in order" for them to respond in like manner.

Nothing could be farther from the truth. Reprisal is a serious demonstration of negative energy and the power of its destructiveness. Frequently the perpetrator of the angry and vengeful feelings and actions is the one who truly suffers most in the outcome because that individual's energy field becomes weakened and moves toward self-destruction. Whenever you make the positive choice toward love, forgiveness, and release of the negative, your energy field lightens and clears the path for higher forms or levels of living.

Why do so many people spend entire lifetimes agonizing over what they perceive another has "done to them"? They lack true understanding of the "opportunity" presented to them for growth by the making and taking of appropriate choices and actions. Everything begins in your mental and emotional perceptions. How do you choose to react or respond initially—in several hours, days, months, and years? If an initial decision to lash out in anger occurs, this negative energy can be reversed easily and quickly as soon as you make the choice to do so. You can accomplish this by a simple word, thought, or even feeling. It can become an automatic process eventually as follows:

❦ You experience a negative emotion, thought, or feeling as a result of something someone has said or done (usually directed toward you or someone close to you).

❦ This feeling intensifies.

❦ You get the impulse to "do something."

❦ You may lash out in anger or keep your feelings repressed

inside of you. Or you may present a cool façade, denying your deep inner resentment.

What are the choices here involving forgiveness?

You can continue in your negative, angry, resentful, revengeful mode with the inherent possibility of causing potential harm to yourself.

You can choose to release this negative energy and replace it with the energy that will make you open, clear, and receptive to learning, growth, and higher living.

How do you actually accomplish the act of letting go or forgiveness or release? Once the decision or inclination to do so becomes apparent, it is easy. The challenge is in recognizing the opportunity presented.

You are aware of your negative or uncomfortable feelings because you may experience strong physical sensations such as reddening of the face, increased heart rate, tightness, anxiety, or fear resulting in trembling. Some may feel a strong desire to strike out with fists or tongues. Many possibilities can occur to make you aware of your intense feelings concerning another.

At this point you can train yourself to make a choice by first recognizing and acknowledging that how you feel is considered normal in today's society.

Take some deep breaths which will help calm you and give you the opportunity to do some introspective searching within yourself.

At this point it is important to remain fully conscious, in the present, and make a decision as to what you desire as your ultimate outcome. Do you choose to go beyond the negativity and resulting discomfort and potential harm to yourself? Or do you choose self-destruction which is the inevitable result of contained resentment?

❀ It is recommended, of course, that you choose the forgiving action.

What does this entail?

❀ Staying present and conscious, you can say to yourself, "I choose to release this negative, detrimental feeling."

❀ You then ask yourself how you will feel when this negative sensation is gone. Experiment by first imagining the negative reaction in your "mind's eye" and then conceiving how it feels to be free of this feeling. Then you choose which feels better to you. By saying a simple word such as **"release,"** you can speed up the process.

Releasing is a natural, spontaneous act that, when willingly entered into, is most gratifying and creates a light, free bodily sensation. Once you experience how wonderful this feels as opposed to oppressive, heavy, negative energy, the decision becomes easy by comparison. Whatever you choose is your freewill choice and is for your learning process.

After you have done this process a few times, you will be able to shift the energy automatically—without a thought. You may use the assistance of a word such as "release," "change," or "clear" to assist you to trigger the shift of energy.

Eventually your total being understands your intention to be light and free and clear, and the process begins occurring even before the initial precipitating event has been completed. You have made your decision to respond by letting go before the negativity can affect you. This is true growth and accomplishment. You then make it possible to live, act, and breath in a state of free, forgiving love and bliss, and it is easier and more gratifying than you ever imagined. All you have to do is be responsibly aware during this process from initial cause to conclusion. You achieve ultimate peace and obtain freedom from the negative effects of what *only you* can "do to yourself" by choosing the inappropriate reaction of resentment. Whenever you choose forgiveness the whole world benefits. This will be discussed further because it is an entire subject in itself. Remember that freewill choice is yours—to forgive or not to forgive—the result being freedom or pain.

# Release *for* Life

**R**ELEASING IS OF COURSE related to forgiveness (or letting go), but it is far more complex. In the subtle sense you may have a clear idea of what this entails. You may visualize it as a going forward and leaving something behind, but this is only part of the picture. Release in a more expansive sense involves commitment to becoming all you can be because once the releasing process is completed, freedom and unlimitedness are the end results. This freedom also entails responsibility. The responsibility is initially to yourself, but ultimately it is greater and more far reaching than to only yourself. The magical tapestry of who you are begins to unveil itself when all that was holding you back is handled. Commitment can be a challenging concept because most people have their individual idea of its true meaning. Yet it is a necessary ingredient in the releasing process.

Commitment first and foremost is to yourself. You must commit to being the best you can be. How can this be accomplished if you're clutching on to old garbage or excess baggage that is holding you back? First of all everything that no longer works positively in your life must be sprung from your consciousness as soon as possible. What do you truly need to keep with you from the past? What from yesterday is presently of benefit to you and/or mankind? Sort this out in your heart and mind. What you choose to retain must be done so with purity of purpose and integrity. What you choose to release must be let go of as quickly as possible after the decision is made. Whatever new considerations then enter your life may be either accepted or rejected according to your truth. Any hesitancy to release represents an unwillingness to give up the old, and this is where *defense mechanisms* enter. Whenever you hesitate to move forward, a backwards step is taken. When this occurs, negative energy is presented with an open door or opportunity to reenter and gain control. There is no possible way to maintain balance and grow if positive choice is not your chosen path.

Whenever you encounter a dilemma or situation in which you do not feel ready to release the old, that is of course your freewill choice. There is no judgment concerning this—only results. What you may experience is stress and stagnation, and soon you may wonder why your life is not working. In reflecting upon their lives, individuals usually can relay to you exactly what is holding them back. They may include negative thoughts and emotions, old belief patterns, inappropriate habits or actions, and lack of positive action. Why does anyone choose these various forms of self-sabotage? Usually there is a feeling of fear or uncertainty of what the future will be like without the burden. Ironically, the excess baggage can help to create a temporary feeling of comfort (through habitual past experience) although discomfort may be the end result. Familiarity can produce a certain level of contentment; however, when you consistently choose to remain stationary in this dubious "comfort zone" instead of moving forward, the total human energy system stagnates and may even shut down.

How do you achieve the level of consciousness which enables you to get control, examine the choices, and move forward? Remember, the decision is always your freewill choice!

✿ First you must be aware that something in your life is not working. You may feel dissatisfaction and frustration, or perhaps you cannot uncover your true life purpose.

✳ The next realization is that something needs to change.

✳ You may be consciously and acutely aware of the negative baggage which is holding you back—or you may not have a clue.

✳ In any case, it may now be time to make a commitment to getting rid of what has no positive purpose in your life. If something is not providing happiness, freedom, and joy, then what use does it hold for you? If it is providing protection in the form of a defense mechanism, perhaps there is a more positive way of achieving the desired result.

✳ Choose now and choose wisely.

✳ Release can occur almost automatically when a sincere decision is reached. It may assist you to verbally express your desire such as, "I now choose to release _____ from my life."

✳ At this point imagine, in your mind's eye, the entire release in the full-blown form, symbol, or picture of whatever was holding you back. See it leaving your body and the surrounding energy field and evaporating into nothingness. Use whatever symbols appeal to you.

✳ Now deep within you feel a new freedom, a wonderful sensation of lightness, as though the bonds or ropes that had been restraining you were now cut, and you truly are free!

What is the other option? Becoming eternally stuck in self-sabotage and maybe even being pulled backwards to a point at which you function at an even lower level is the downside result of choosing to hold on to old baggage.

Assuming you embrace the decision to release and do so, what do you do with your new found freedom? You have gained much additional time for productivity because you are free from all the hours previously engaged in worry, concern, self-sabotage, and self- pity.

How do you move forward? Most people, when asked, can verbalize a myriad of things they have always wanted to do, be, or have. You now have unlimited and unencumbered freedom to pursue these objectives. It can be a very simple desire or a lifetime's work. It doesn't matter at all what it is—whether it is great or small in concept. What is important is that now you are free to pursue anything without the past holding you back. If you do not have a desire you are aware of, that is fine too. You are now free to be open to one coming in. You may have been so involved in previously holding on to your excess baggage that not much else could enter your life. Rest in the knowledge that all will come to you at the appropriate time and when you are ready. Relax and have no judgment as to what or when or how important. Maybe the optimum circumstance for you at this point is to just enjoy your new found feeling of freedom.

You may want to go out into nature to observe and experience what freedom feels like. In the great outdoors you are without emotional tugs and ties, and you truly get a sense of how all natural things effortlessly flow. It is easier to align with *your* true nature—your true self, and quite often inspiration and insights will come to you.

What is essential is to be open to receive these creative influences so you can recognize and act upon them. You may assist this process by asking yourself questions such as, "How do I feel?" "What do I want to be different?" Then it is a matter of time and dedication to let the desires mature in your mind as you commit to their creation in your life. Each day now you are free to take a step or two forward in achieving the goal or desire because what previously held you back has disappeared because you willed it. Each day you feel stronger and more powerful because you have overcome. If you can accomplish this, what more can you do?

When you experience the simple act of releasing, you realize it was much more difficult to hang on to what you did not need in your life than to let it go. You were unaware in the past because you were stuck in an old habit or way of thinking (or held onto a false belief belonging to you to or someone else who passed it on to you). At the time you were not able to see the light. Now you can, and you are free because you made the simple but important and necessary choice to "let it go."

You may know of others who are immobilized due to the holding on of old attitudes, beliefs, emotions, or even "things" that clutter their lives. When you encounter them, feel grateful that you have gone beyond. If they ask what you do to make your life work, share with them your process of release. In the "sharing" you become even more fulfilled, and you open yourself up to receiving additional methods and inspirations for your growth.

Be true to yourself, and let go of all that no longer works.

# Recognition for Life

**RECOGNITION IS SOMETIMES** defined as acknowledgment or receiving praise or appreciation for work or accomplishments. In this sense it is something many individuals desire at one time or another. Most people, and perhaps you, like to feel noticed or "special" every once in a while. This is considered normal when it occurs in proper balance in relation to everything else going on in your life. However it is often the case that the desire for recognition becomes inflated out of proportion. When this happens a state of imbalance is the result. How you relate and respond to the hunger for recognition is of essence.

When you perform a good deed with a pure heart and the genuine motive of assisting another or coming to the aid of someone in need, recognition is theoretically in order but not expected. The act is executed automatically and spontaneously—free of a preconceived desire for acknowledgment or gratification. Recognition is the end result, but to you, the perpetrator of the positive or kind action, it was never the motivation. The action was pure in intention and completed in love because you were operating from your heart where motives are pure.

Pure acts of love and kindness are done without thought or deliberation. They can be as simple as running to open a door for an individual encumbered in some way, or they can be as challenging as jumping into freezing cold water to save the life of a drowning child. Your heart and inner being just "knows" this is what you "must" do with no thought as to your convenience, comfort, or personal safety. The needs of the other take precedence. A personal motive in this instance does not exist to any degree in your heart or mind as you perform the benevolent action.

This is, of course, not natural or automatic in regard to many people. It may instead be normal to hesitate, with the mind running a gamut of excuses, or pretending to be unaware of the need of another. Whenever this occurs, it's like the ostrich burying its head in the sand. There is no judgment here because everyone has the freewill choice to act or not to act. What is of consequence is the result of that freewill choice.

Is it better to act in a positive way automatically or as a result of mental evaluation and decision making? There is no judgment once again, but those with a higher level of consciousness and alignment with their higher being are the ones who choose spontaneous right action according to their elevated values. Their motives are always pure, and recognition as an end result is "out of the picture." In fact, the true "good deed" perpetrators often disappear before being acknowledged or thanked. These are the individuals who perform good deeds anonymously. Their motives are in being kind or helpful, not in achieving recognition or praise.

What about the individual who is motivated by praise and recognition? This can be a positive inducement in achieving personal success, providing the desire remains in proper proportion. Athletes, scholars, and those with high level careers are often driven to achieve by the lure of reward, and this is appropriate when kept in balance with the other aspects of life.

A negative situation arises when an individual plans and calculates actions or even creates false scenarios in order to receive attention or recognition. Often this occurs at the expense of another, becomes extremely out of proportion, and the person is thrown out of balance. The driving force was for a negative goal, in essence.

You are presented with many opportunities each day to be aware and to pay attention in order to see where you and your actions lie. What are your motivations for positive action? Do you, in fact, perform positive action? What **IS** positive action? All is determined by your own personal perception.

Following are a few guidelines you can use to gain better understanding of yourself and your position in relation to your growth.

❀ The first step is to be aware and be willing to stand to the side "in your mind" and take a non-judgmental, objective look at yourself, your actions, and your motivations to "act" or "not to act."

❀ When a situation presents itself and provides the opportunity for a decision, what happens as you observe? Notice the feelings or emotions in your physical body. What thoughts run through your head?

❀ Notice if you are immobilized by thought and indecision or if you act automatically without thought or analysis of the situation. Does your action represent the best intention possible, or do you hide, turn away, or pretend you are unaware?

How do you make a positive decision if you are one who evaluates prior to action?

❀ First of all, put yourself into the situation in your mind's eye. Imagine yourself performing first positively and then negatively.

❀ Ask yourself which action feels better.

Now you know which path of action creates the most balance for you. Freewill choice still exists, and you learn, and you learn, and you learn.

What about those individuals who act for the sole purpose of praise? Insecurity may be a motivating force. Ego can enter in as well. Can true reward ever be experienced when the motive is not pure and the action not undertaken with love? What do you think? How do you feel about this? Remember that everything you encounter is for the purpose of learning, growing, and evolving.

Recognition earned without preconceived desire is on an entirely different level from connived greed for praise. Where do you wish to be in relation to a choice between the two? You are free to move from the negative to the positive at any given moment. All that is required is a freewill decision to do so at the time it is most appropriate. Eventually you will choose the more positive path. It's similar to breaking an old pattern or habit, and your own personal time frame is your decision.

Ultimate recognition, therefore, comes to you from the greatest source—that inner knowing and feeling of appropriateness, balance, and harmony deep inside. This far supersedes any acknowledgment obtained from others or via any external source. Listen to your inner voice which assists you to recognize your true and correct action at all times.

# Validation for Life

 **HEREAS RECOGNITION** might give you a feeling of honor or praise, validation is a much stronger and more powerful concept. Validation becomes significant when you do not feel worthy or adequate unless validated by another person.

Few children are unconditionally affirmed by parents, teachers, and other prominent authority figures during their formative years. Consequently they can grow up feeling lost, disjointed, or even unworthy. Why is this so? The human psyche is not created to run independently in a vacuum, free from the influence of others because it is through the mirror image in another's eyes that you see yourself. That is, what is characteristic for you is seen in another. Whenever you are in the company of others and still feel good about yourself, that means you are validated.

An important goal is the concept of self-validation, although few achieve it. Why do people always seem to look to others rather than to their own inner being for self-discovery? For one thing it feels safer because many people have lost the belief in themselves that is necessary for true self-validation. Where did the false idea originate that someone else knows better than **YOU?** It began in ancient times when people lost the ability to heal themselves, or so they thought. This is not true; however, they felt that others were more powerful than themselves so they began going to them for advice and healing of all forms. They believed what other people told them at the expense of their own knowledge and belief concerning themselves. They even began to make important life changes and decisions according to what some outsider recommended.

The question concerning giving up personal power to others is that if the advice turns out to be incorrect, who is responsible—the individual giving the advice or the one following it? Why would you ever believe that someone else knows better what is appropriate for you! This concept applies to all areas of life.

There are advisors and counselors who guide people into education, careers, marriages, child-rearing practices, health practices, and various other areas according to their own beliefs, knowledge, and experience. If you blindly follow their advice without question, what does this indicate? It means that you have relinquished your power or confidence in making your own decisions to another person. The person who you consult can in no conceivable way know all that is involved concerning you or always be able to recommend the optimal course of action. What if you are here to learn self-discipline and someone consistently tells you the "easy way out"? An outsider can never totally grasp the intensity of your inner feelings or extent of your inner knowing. Although you may be aware that your inner guidance is ever present and accurate, do you trust the advice of another rather than believing in yourself to make your own valid choices? No one on earth can guide you through life better than the inner you. When not used, this natural inner guidance steps into the background, and the voice becomes softer and softer until some individuals completely lose touch with their inner knowing.

How can you reconnect with your own inner knower or advisor to regain your power and self-validation?

⚜ First be aware and believe that all your answers lie within your own being.

✿ Then begin to listen to the advice you are hearing. To do this you must quiet the chatter of your mind which can create the fears and doubts that cause you to lose trust and belief in yourself. Sitting quietly in silence assists you to hear your inner voice. Often you won't hear actual words, but you may gain an insight or receive an inspiration or just have a strong impulse or feeling about something or someone in your life. It is helpful to focus your attention in the upper portion of your head during this process.

✿ When you receive an impulse to take an action and you follow it, that means you have begun to establish your own self-validation and have taken the responsibility for your life back into your own hands. The more you follow the direction of your own inner voice, the louder the voice will become.

✿ Eventually you respond to all aspects of your life automatically and spontaneously by just "knowing" what is appropriate for you. Your own intuitive guidance far supersedes what any person outside yourself can offer you. Of course, it is appropriate to obtain knowledge from others who have specialized in various endeavors and learned technology and wide ranges of mastered skills. When you seek to learn from their information, what is important is to have a deep feeling within your being whether or not what they say feels appropriate for **YOU**. It may be adequate or correct for others but not for you. The answer must come from your true inner knowing. You are used to evaluating, analyzing, and making important decisions with your intellect. The decisions made through pure intellectual thought are only your "half" truth. Your "full" truth can only come from your inner truth and knowing.

✿ When you master self-validation as an automatic process, you move into an arena in which your life works much better. You will feel more and more comfort in your life, and your strength of character will increase.

Why has this subject been emphasized? Multitudes of people are running around like chickens with their heads cut off—lost, without direction, and not knowing their next step. They may spend weeks, months, years, or a lifetime searching for the answers and following numerous blind or inappropriate paths. Remember that no one can advise you better than **YOU YOURSELF**.

What happens when you have an inner knowing or feeling and reject it or take an alternate or even opposite direction? Have you ever said, "I knew I should have done such and such," or "I knew I should not have gone there," or "I wish I had followed my first impulse"? When you have these reflections on past opportunities or experiences, you are receiving a strong message to pay attention in the future. Ignoring the most precious guidance you own can spell disaster. Following this perfection within can bring magic, joy, self-confidence, strength, and power along with self-validation into your life. Trust that in the area of decision making, **YOU ARE ALL YOU NEED**. You may be guided by your inner voice to seek knowledge or information from others, and if this occurs, only then is it appropriate. Another individual may have a piece of information or expertise which is useful to you. When you receive it, however, go within to validate it for you and your life. Every time you do so you become more your true self. Validate **SELF**, not others, in order to be all you can be.

# Rejection for Life

**A**T ONE TIME OR another almost all individuals, and most likely you, have felt rejected. This often begins early in childhood when you were not allowed to participate in an event because of being "too young" or "too small." Even certain carnival rides require that children be measured and must be a certain height in order to be allowed on the ride.

Then you go to school and discover that only specified people are chosen as friends or called on by the teacher to answer questions or receive special favors. What happens as a result is that you may develop feelings of inadequacy and unworthiness. Self-esteem takes a dive, and sometimes the outcome is a life-long struggle. If you get the message as a young child that you are not acceptable to others, there is underlying danger that you might become unacceptable to yourself.

Self-rejection is one of the most traumatic aspects to overcome in the personality because it affects all areas of your life. How can you formulate a successful relationship with another individual if you are at odds with yourself? This is why so many marriages break up. The self-rejecting partner projects this heavy energy of rejection into the midst of the relationship.

What can be done in this situation? Once and for all, the message is always **LOVE**—to love and accept yourself, a prerequisite to loving and accepting others. Although you may initially believe it is easier said than done, all that is required is a change of consciousness—being aware of your true nature rather than the false idea that was imposed upon you against your will or without your knowledge at an earlier time. What is essential is for you to take control and say to yourself, "I choose to change." When the sincere desire to **FEEL** and **BE** different comes into play, you are then open to various avenues of assistance.

You now begin to examine who you truly are. This is sometimes referred to as "finding oneself." There are numerous books and classes to assist you, but much or most of the work must be done by you alone in silent inner communication. In the quiet peaceful calmness of your solitude, begin to look at yourself from a different point of view. Reflect on the positive traits that are an intrinsic part of you. You have accomplished innumerable important things, learned, and participated in many positive areas of expression. Take a few moments to review some of your successes and talents. It is always beneficial to keep your positive aspects in the forefront. The habit of rejecting the self or a part of the self is only an imaginary occurrence concocted by the mind although it presents itself as being very real.

In essence self-rejection can exist only in your mind. It is done by you and you alone regardless of what others may have done to you, and you can rise above it just by changing your consciousness.

How do you do that?

❦ First you are aware of the unhappy or depressing feelings you have concerning yourself. You may or may not be cognizant of the source of these feelings of rejection. It does not matter.

❦ Imagine how you would like to feel about yourself, and step into new shoes of self-acceptance and self-love. Examine how that would feel.

❦ If you prefer these positive feelings and attitudes, make the choice and commitment to yourself to create the change in your being. Only you can make this happen.

❦ After choosing to participate in transforming yourself, the most important thing is to do so at your own pace. Some people will transform the negative into the positive immediately with ease and enthusiasm. They have a sudden enlightened insight that it is an easy process and merely consists of changing their thought and reaction patterns. Others may choose a long, drawn-out process of self-determination and experience many ups and downs in their self-analysis (or analysis by others) before reaching the end goal of self-acceptance.

❦ It is essential to continuously monitor your thoughts and feelings concerning yourself. You can be aware of your bodily sensations and be on guard for any discomfort. If any old feelings of self-doubt, low self-esteem, or blatant rejection creep in out of old habit patterns, you can stop them instantly.

❦ To change the energy to the positive, all you have to do is say a word such as "change" or "transform" forcefully and imagine the negative energy as a cloud quickly evaporating.

❦ Then you recreate the positive feelings of self-acceptance and self-worth merely by sensing how it truly is to feel good about yourself.

❦ Intensify the positive feelings and spend a few moments experiencing the increased strength and happiness that result.

❦ Remember that you are in charge of how you choose to feel about yourself at any given time. Your true self deserves to be accepted and loved.

Some people express concern that it is inappropriate to "love yourself"—that egomania is a possible outcome. This is not what is being addressed here. Loving yourself is a matter of honoring the beauty and perfection of who you really are. Only the mind can dispel self-love which was the original intent and your birthright, and only the mind can recreate it in your life. Do not look to others to do it for you.

You can see a reflection of who you truly are when you venture out into nature and experience the many facets of beauty and perfection that exist there. Feel the majesty of the trees and receive from them the idea of "self-support." Observe the cascading waterfalls and experience "strength, power, and sense of purpose." Notice the water in babbling brooks and streams and perceive the continuous flow of all life, including yours specifically. Search out the flowers and plants, mountains, oceans, meadows, forests, and all aspects of nature. Relate all of these elements of nature one-by-one to sensations you can incorporate inside yourself. Give each a symbol, and then become what they represent. They are part of you, and you are part of them. Therefore you can assist your growth by adding the beautiful and pure elements of nature to your presence by merely incorporating the feelings they give you when you allow yourself access to them.

Be still within your own inner being and know that nature does not reject itself. It follows the natural pattern of birth, death, and seasons, but it always accepts itself. Become like the beauty you see because it is in the choosing that this is accomplished. You then free yourself from fear, self-doubt, and discomfort in your body.

When you feel "out of sorts" with yourself, recall your favorite spot in nature and bring back the sensations that place inspires into your body. Experience the acceptance and love this place holds for you. Bring it into your body, mind, and spirit, and make it yours. The choice for self-acceptance and self-love becomes natural and normal once you see clearly and disassociate from old negative impressions falsely acquired in the past. Choose love, and you and your relationships will flourish. The choice is yours. The reward is life without struggle.

# Spontaneity *for Life*

*L*IFE TODAY ENCOMPASSES many rules and regulations, a great number of which are self-imposed. In the past from "day one," babies used to be put on a strict feeding schedule by well-meaning doctors who thought that eating "not one minute before every four hours" was necessary and appropriate. Mothers would wait in agony listening to the sounds of their crying infants until the appointed moment. Although many babies thrive on routine, some degree of flexibility may have been in order.

Early programmed agendas were followed by years of scheduled school, play, and work hours. Eventually you became accustomed to observing your clock or wristwatch continuously throughout the day, being dictated to by two revolving hands on a face of numbers or a digital display of minutes and seconds. You may still feel you cannot have dinner until "dinner time" or retire for the night until it is "bedtime."

How did you become entangled in this non-serving system of clock watching? By observing and copying what everyone else did, you unconsciously became a slave to some external force. Once again it involves giving up your power—not to a living, breathing person but to a mechanical instrument. How many times a day do you look at your wristwatch and clock or ask someone what time it is? How often are you stopped by some-one else inquiring of you the hour?

Of course order rather than chaos is a precipitating cause for your involvement with time, and scheduled hours are appropri-ate for certain things. For instance, what would happen if all the television stations aired their various programs simultaneously without a planned schedule? The result would be a static blur.

Airplane take-offs and landings must be regulated for the pro-tection and safety of all. A list of necessary or appropriate sched-uling does exist; however, what in your life can be changed and improved by loosening up the rigid routine of your waking hours?

One of the major habitual daily events is sleep time. Have you ever said or heard someone say, "I'm sleepy, but it's too early to go to bed"? Consequently the need to sleep is not hon-ored, and you stay up yawning without enjoyment. Then morn-ing arrives, and the alarm rings before you feel you have had enough sleep. You are not ready to awaken, but the clock says you must. The snooze alarm represents an invention to assist you to balance your inclination to sleep a few additional pre-cious moments with the sense of urgency to get up and begin your day. It can cause one more irritation and infringes on your true inner clock which knows exactly what time is appropriate for retiring and awakening.

What is the point of all this discussion? When so much of your life is governed by external forces, it is easy to lose sight of who you are in the scheme of things and also of what is appro-priate for you to do at any particular moment. Whenever you become a slave to an artificial creation such as a clock, you can-not live perfectly in the moment. It is challenging to be where your inner self wants you to be—doing what is appropriate for you to do when the "clock" dictates that you need to be some-where else, doing or participating in another pre-arranged activ-ity. Thus you feel torn between the part of you which knows what is your truth in the moment and the part that is manipu-lated by outside forces.

This might appear to be an unsolvable dilemma. What are some things you can do to recover the spontaneity of life? Do you even remember the last time you had a wonderful experience of spontaneity? Perhaps someone called you "at the last minute" and invited you to go somewhere. Although you had a long list of things to do, you instantly agreed to go, feeling quite impulsive, and you had a marvelous time. How about the time you all of a sudden decided to leave your stack of paperwork and refresh yourself in an activity you preferred? Hopefully, you felt exhilarated, liberated, and rejuvenated rather than guilty.

There is a difference between feeling responsible to do the appropriate thing at the appointed hour and guilty if you do not fulfill the plan exactly. It is recommended that you search your inner feelings to discover which course of action is appropriate for you at all times. What is this procedure?

- First you become aware that you desire to do something or go somewhere.

- Immediately you sense conflict because your clock or calendar says, "No, you need to be somewhere else or be involved in another activity."

- Negatively, you could make yourself miserable by weighing both options, evaluating and analyzing the situation without resolution. A positive approach would be to place yourself "in your mind's eye" first into the scenario of what you desire and sense how that feels. Secondly, do the same with the obligatory alternative choice. Which feels preferable at an inner level?

- Make the decision to choose what feels best. You will not know consciously until you have actually completed this process. The result or determination may surprise you.

- Carry out and fulfill your inner-guided desire whatever it is, free of guilt, second guessing, or looking back.

The constant and endless mind chatter is what prevents peo-ple from spontaneity and realizing all that life has to offer. It is important to pause and say, "I'm feeling something unusual, and I need to recognize it." Each individual may have a slightly dif-ferent idea of the appropriate course of action. When you check out your true inner guidance and spontaneously follow the advice without analyzing and evaluating, then you are in bal-ance with your true self, your inherent nature, which always knows what is most suitable for you. When you trust and follow these inner feelings, you become more and more balanced, and you also become exceedingly secure within yourself. You have taken your power back!

Spontaneity can initially cause some conflict within yourself or in relations with others, but when you establish your own inner power and belief in yourself by following your heart, the power of the conflict will evaporate. Your truth and inner guid-ance become all powerful and more important than any clock or external demand made upon you. Follow your heart and spon-taneity will follow. All preconceived repercussions, fears, and innuendos of guilt vanish as you take control of your life by spontaneous "intuitive action." You will recognize your full magnitude and experience a quantum leap in growth when you realize you are almost floating through life—in balance because every cell of your body is in harmony with the knowledge that you are true to yourself and innermost spontaneous impulses. There is that part inside you that guides you perfectly at all times to be and do what is appropriate. Joy and bliss are the result. Put the mind to the side and follow your heart to achieve spontaneous ideal life and living. You can do it!

# Freewill Choice *for Life*

**U**P TO THIS POINT, freewill choice has been referred to in this book and touched on in passing. Now it is time to expand and expound on this subject because many individuals do not truly understand what it is—let alone believe they possess it.

Continuously throughout the day you exercise your freewill choice. When you open your eyes and decide to get out of bed in the morning, you make one of your very first daily freewill choices. Some of your choices virtually become habits, and you aren't even conscious of them. Seldom do you hesitate and reflect, "I have a freewill choice here." Usually you unconsciously put yourself on automatic until an event or occurrence presents itself in such a way to demand your attention.

Often some form of uncertainty or conflict emerges which creates an awareness that there is a choice to be made, and it may involve temptation. Temptation represents a tendency or desire to do something deemed inappropriate by your innermost being, your true self. When temptation presents itself, you have the choice of overcoming or submitting. Herein lies an expanded opportunity for growth. If you find that the same temptation arises time and time again, you can be sure it is one you need to pay careful attention to now. This represents an area you need to explore and heal for your own personal growth. It could be anything ranging from simple overeating to any other more complex or addictive behavior of greater intensity and effect on your life. Whether or not you realize it, each temptation provides an opportunity for growth. What role does freewill choice play?

❦ The temptation presents itself.

❦ You become aware that you desire something.

❦ Your mind immediately begins its chatter as you become aware that part of you is drawn in one direction and another part is bent toward the other, usually opposite direction.

❦ You are aware that the inclination you are most attracted to (in being tempted) may also have a tingling of discomfort associated with it. This is known as guilt. The more appropriate choice for you may not contain the feeling of "excitement" or "charge" the less appropriate desire presents.

❦ Now you are most likely torn by your feelings. You may proceed on "automatic" or go "unconscious" (not in the literal sense) and jump into the desired behavior without further consideration. Or, at this point, the conflict may increase in intensity in your mind.

❦ Sooner or later a choice is made. Let us shortcut the issue and suggest a positive method of choosing. Once again as previously described, run the two options through your imagination, taking time to truly feel from an inner level which one is overall most appropriate and empowering for you.

When it comes to free will, however, your choice is truly *your* choice. Usually no one "forces" you to make the majority of decisions in your life although you may have to cope with a considerable amount of advice from others. You may have discovered that many people believe they know what is best for you. Why is this? They search their own value and belief systems and relay to you their innermost underlying constructs which are appropriate to them. This has **NOTHING** to do with you at your inner level of truth. Others may mean well and offer advice from the best intentions and highest level of which they are capable, but this may have nothing to do with you at your core level. In essence "they" are not "you," and they can only in truth choose for themselves. They are not ultimately responsible for your choices and would often do well to keep their opinions to themselves.

An appropriate time for interference does exist, however, in the case of parents interacting with their very young children. The children have not fully developed their judgment and value systems, and parents may need to intervene to prevent possible injury. The young child needs parental guidance to a certain extent. Eventually, however, the parents must step to the side in order for the child to learn and grow according to his or her freewill choices. This may not be the parents' preference and often represents a challenging concept to grasp and integrate. Parents feel responsibility (often significantly out of proportion) for their children's actions and decisions.

How can this issue be resolved? When the child in the formative years is presented with a decision, he or she does not have enough knowledge or complete awareness of possible outcomes. It is appropriate for parents to point these out. The caution, however, as the child matures is to refrain from making your own personal judgments in relation to the child's choices. Ultimately the child must learn through the outcomes of his or her choices. If the child is unhappy with the consequences of his or her decisions or actions, then valuable learning has been gained. The next choice may be considered in a different light—the light of experience. This is the beginning of enlightened choices—the path to enlightenment which is pursued by everyone, consciously or unconsciously.

What can "enlightened choices" provide for you? The answer is quite simple. Your life becomes easier and free from struggle. The more frequently you make appropriate decisions which shall be referred to as "enlightened choices," this process becomes increasingly automatic, and your inner voice speaks to you with greater volume and clarity as you respond and follow your highest impulses. You begin to ignore the old mind chatter which eventually loses its power over you and its past ability to both tempt you and make you feel guilty. What is most rewarding is that you have gotten to this point by making freewill, enlightened choices. You rise to higher and higher levels of awareness as you are presented with more challenging opportunities for growth through choice.

In the beginning you dealt with the basics for survival. As you become more enlightened through freewill choice, you come into your own true power. What does this mean? You no longer have the need to ask others' opinions because you learn to trust your own inner guidance, impulses, and messages which result in correct choices for you. Realize that your choices may not be the appropriate ones for anyone else, but if they are correct for you, then they are your truth.

You will experience increased strength and power when you reach the point and come to the realization that you no longer are even "tempted" to ask for advice or opinions from others. You have learned by this time that, although well intended, advice from others is not connected to (or a reflection of) your truth. You may also have experienced negative outcomes resulting from taking the advice or following the opinions of others. Only you can know what is appropriate for you, and you are responsible for following your own inner advice "to you." The outcome is growth and learning. Greater opportunities will be presented to you the more you exercise enlightened freewill choice.

On the other hand, let us examine freewill choice from a different view. What if you make a choice that is negative or inappropriate? Is this not in order? What if you continuously seek others' opinions, submitting to their truth and advice rather than your own? Refrain from judging yourself because this may be your perfect path and personal process of self-discovery, and ultimately you will ascertain what needs to be mastered.

All individuals have freewill choice. Everyone attracts various and unique experiences depending on their needs and level of consciousness. Freewill choice merely provides pathways for growth as you learn from the results of your decisions. The secret is to take charge of those choices and consult your heart as well as the possible outcomes. Freewill choice is your gift from the Universe. Appreciate it.

# Commitment for Life

**C**OMMITMENT TO YOURSELF is the primary requirement and basis for growth and personal evolution. It may be far easier to commit to your career, family, or some external creation or activity than to yourself. Commitment to self also involves a true dedication to fulfilling your life's purpose. First, of course, you must discover exactly what that objective is. Some individuals are here principally to balance the energy rather than to be action oriented. Nevertheless, everyone has a mission or purpose.

How do you discover your mission? Herein lies the key to self-awareness and the resulting self-commitment.

- First of all it is essential to quiet the mind once again because it is full of "shoulds" and opinions of your purpose or mission. This can be done by sitting silently with eyes closed in a meditative state.

- Ask to see yourself (in your imagination) doing something or being somewhere. Expand your awareness and intend to receive the information.

- Notice what images, ideas, or words first come into your awareness.

These are indications that may symbolize either a purpose or desire you need to consider fulfilling for yourself.

If at this point you receive insight into a course of action that feels positive to you, you may do well to pay very close attention. When you put a large share of your energy toward pursuing an intent, whatever it is, you seem to magically receive help and guidance out of "nowhere." When you become 100% committed, all the forces of the Universe seem to rally behind you to create opportunities and provide the means for successful completion.

Great joy manifests on all levels when you see and experience the magic in your life resulting from commitment. Dedication to a goal can be all encompassing, so let's return now to what was originally referred to as "commitment to yourself."

Commitment to yourself essentially means steadfast devotion to your own truth in face of anything that may interfere with it. You must be strong in your beliefs and trust in yourself and your inner guidance because without this you can be swayed or diverted by external influences. Then your commitment to self would lack sincerity and resemble "half truths." Only when commitment to self is 100% does your life work perfectly for you. Resist holding out on yourself or succumbing to putting your priorities on the back burner.

You may possibly be thinking that this sounds like a self-centered or selfish concept. In reality it is not because once you live a life of commitment to yourself, you also come into balance with universal forces. When this alignment occurs you can venture with greater strength and power into any place or activity and put forth the effort required to more effectively assist others in their projects or plans if that is appropriate for you. This process in itself becomes rewarding and fulfilling. You are always assured of continually being presented with opportunities.

Once you, even as a child, truly committed yourself to becoming or doing the "best you could," it was possible to be the star pitcher on the softball team, win the art contest, or receive an

"A" on a school project. The greater the commitment, the greater the reward. Sometimes the reward or compensation is simply the inner knowing that you have done your best or put your "all" into an endeavor. Whatever the outcome, your committed participation is what really counts.

What if a situation arises in which your head tells you to take part but your heart is not 100% supportive, or you may actually not want to participate at all? What is the appropriate course of action?

🎋 Silence your mind.

🎋 Envision yourself performing the activity half-heartedly (without commitment).

🎋 Imagine how this would feel.

🎋 Picture yourself rejecting or refraining from the activity, and experience how that would feel.

It now becomes easier to make the decision. If it feels better to avoid being involved in an activity or situation rather than to enter into it against your desire, the appropriate choice is obviously apparent. You can quickly become out of balance and harmony with yourself and others every time you do something that does not feel totally correct to you. This can occur at a very subtle energy level as well, so pay close attention to the signals your body, mind, and spirit send to you.

Many individuals consent to do things to which they are not fully committed. Others experience a "sense" of self blame and guilt if they turn people down. Who are you undermining or harming in the long run? It is only you who can permit yourself to feel guilty. Although you will encounter others who will attempt to place a guilt trip on you, when you live in your truth and grant yourself permission to be 100% self-committed, you will no longer be affected by them. You will realize that the greatest gift you can give (other than love) is being committed and true to yourself. Your experiences become positive, supportive, and empowering as you correspondingly stimulate truth and awareness for others.

You become a role model of strength, power, and confidence. Others will want to know your secret when they see the results in your life. Share what you have learned because in the sharing you also grow as well as achieving even higher levels of self-expression and commitment.

Once self-commitment is firmly established in your consciousness, commitment to other people or activities remains in balance, and your life flows smoothly. You are able to keep all responses and actions in proper proportion because of an inner focus that guides you perfectly. Once your roots are established, you come from a place of power and are free to choose how you want to branch out in life. Commit to yourself, and all else falls into place as a natural outcome.

# Transference

**T**RANSFERENCE IS ASSOCIATED with the concept of power being shifted from one individual to another and also between various levels within yourself. Everyone experiences transference at some level in the area of personal power and in responsibility to self and others.

From the time you first begin your job or career, responsibility is allocated to you from an employer unless you are self-employed. Seldom do you attain responsibility at this level without it originating from an outside source. Imagine what it would be like for everyone to be accountable for themselves without receiving, delegating, or transferring power or responsibility to or from others. This would be isolated empowerment in the original or ultimate sense.

Transference also exists within yourself as you climb to higher and higher levels of evolution. Your power increases as does your overall liability for self which will be dealt with in greater detail later.

Small children learn their initial capabilities in response to the demands of parents and authority figures. When they reach school age, more and more is expected of them. They must discipline their minds and physical bodies in order to perform certain tasks. Eventually responsibility is transferred to the inner core level of each individual. When this takes the form of self-motivation, the process of transference has matured and signifies true growth within the self.

Every once in a while you may experience an inkling of these inner processes, although external transference is more obvious and easier to detect. A visible example of external transference occurs in the work place in which a pecking order prevails. It is easy to become lost in the day-to-day challenges of cooperation and competition, and their resulting stresses.

If you are mindful of your inner transference and increase your personal power and level of consciousness, self-empowered living can be yours. Rather than placing your attention on daily frustrations, focus on the growth that results from your challenges. Transfer your attention to a more enlightened level. This can be accomplished by the simple method of choices. Concentrate on what you believe to be to your personal benefit as well as to the greater welfare of mankind. If all of us focus our attention in a positive direction, the entire planet and all inhabiting it will transfer to a more stable existence and improved state of mind.

Exactly what are you asked to do?

- First of all be aware of the forces operating in your life.

- Sense which people or areas of your life are projecting positive or negative vibrations or impressions to you.

- Examine whether or not you are transferring positive or negative vibrations to anyone or anything outside yourself.

- Experience for yourself how this feels at "heart level." This is where your truth lies.

- Determine whether or not you wish to continue in your present mode. Is it beneficial to you and/or others?

- Act upon your decision by taking control of your life and accepting responsibility for yourself. Only you know what is right for you. Follow your heart.

If there is something you need to release, do so—transfer it
out of your life.

Growth in itself is a process of expanding and transferring
your consciousness to greater and greater awareness. Trust in
the natural process of transference to appreciate the magic of
your growth and evolution as well as that of all nature.

Reflect on the mother birds in springtime pushing their babies
out of the nest when it is time for them to learn how to fly. This
also symbolizes transference of power. One tree or plant in the
forest may take precedence over another. Growth provides
numerous avenues, options, and opportunities from which to
choose on the human level. The important thing is to continue
to escalate in your process.

Transference can manifest, it must be cautioned, in a downward cycle, so be alert to the signs designating whether you are
moving upward or downward. What would it feel like if you
were transmitting your power downward? You might be out of
control or experience a feeling of being overly dependent on others or enslaved to their desires or demands. You could suffer
from a sense of frustration, purposelessness, or even exaggerated
stress and anxiety. If you feel at the mercy of others, it is important to do whatever is necessary to recover and regain your own
power and transfer it back to the position of your personal
strength and power. Be grateful, however, for what you have
learned about yourself along the way. It is the awareness that
"things can improve" that will assist and motivate you to take
control. Some individuals choose to wait for a debilitating and
devastating crisis before they transfer their power inward and
upward. It is your choice. The options are being shared with you
to make you aware in just another way that nothing is permanent. All is in a constant state of change and flux. You may
choose to grab hold of the ring and take the ride, allowing what
may come. Or you can transfer all your energies into creating
what you want. This process will be discussed in greater detail
further on. Choice and self-determination belong to you.

Transfer your awareness, decisions, and way of being in the world to what is appropriate for you at any given time. Change is always an option.

# Judgment for Life

**I**F THERE WERE A root of all evil, it would certainly not be money. It would be judgment—judgment of others and, even more serious, judgment of self. Judgment is basically a habit of looking at things in a certain critical way, and it is one of the easiest negative energies to correct. It merely takes being or becoming aware of what you are doing and deciding to respond differently.

Judging exists in society at all levels, and some forms appear to be appropriate and acceptable. There are judges for athletic events and numerous types of contests and competitions. They compare, analyze, and evaluate one individual's performance in relation to another's. Judging presents a challenging role because frequently the decision (or judgment) can be looked upon with disfavor. Why, then, is it considered an honor to be a "judge"? The word alone connotes prestige and generates a feeling of importance. You are most likely aware of the pomp and circumstance of courtroom procedure when a legal judge enters and exits—let alone the intrinsic powerful overtones in the duration he or she is "presiding."

Judging involves making decisions regarding another individual who is more or less helpless to affect the outcome. In other words, you are at the mercy of the judge, and furthermore, this institution of "judges" is a creation of society.

On a personal level, judgments are continuously being made by most people in their everyday lives. From the moment you encounter others, either on your way to work or having arrived at the work place, you observe and judge them. You may criticize someone's driving, appearance, actions, or words. Whatever can be observed can be judged, evaluated, or analyzed. The judgment can be positive, but unfortunately, all too often it is negative.

When you negatively judge another, you are setting yourself up in a position of superiority. Usually you judge others in order to put yourself in a more positive light by comparison. This can occur consciously or unconsciously. Be aware that any negative energy projected from you to another first goes through you and can cause undesirable effects in your body and life.

One of the first steps to be taken by anyone on a path of growth or desiring self-improvement is to put an end to the appraisal of others. If you cannot help noticing unusual aspects of someone else, just "observe" free of judgment or criticism. Be aware that you do not know the history or complete story concerning another, so it would be impossible, even if appropriate, to make a valid judgment.

You do not know the purpose of others nor the appropriate path of growth and learning for them. What you might be tempted to judge harshly in people might actually be perfect for what they need to learn. **YOU** just do not ever have enough information about others to condemn them. People can adequately learn from the results of their experiences (choices and actions and way of being in the world). No one has a need for or benefits from being judged by another (unless of course the benefit is receiving an Olympic Gold Medal). This is not really the slant of this discussion, however.

When you decide to stop judging others, what steps do you take?

🎵 First you need to become aware of when your mental or verbal processes are "judgmental." This may take a while to master and notice on a steady basis because judgment can be a firmly entrenched habit. Judgments often occur instantly and automatically almost like reflexes.

❧ You must constantly monitor your thoughts and impressions to know when you are engaged in judging. This presents a challenge because although judgment is usually negative, the act of judging can make you feel exhilarated, or you may temporarily experience an elevated impression of yourself at the expense of another. You then need to reflect on what has occurred via your thoughts or words in order to become aware that you have participated in the process of judgment.

❧ Now you have the choice of holding on to your judgment (perhaps justifying it to yourself) or letting it go. Releasing judgment is the recommended choice, but as always, you have FREE WILL.

❧ An effective way to end or correct the perceived judgment, or decision of negative context, is to say or think the words, "erase" or "cancel" or "correct." This will stop the energy.

❧ You next need to re-phrase or change your thoughts or words into a positive context. For example, you might be thinking to yourself, "No wonder that woman is so fat, she continuously stuffs her mouth with great amounts of junk food." There are many things you do not know about this woman and the reasons for her actions. She might be going through an emotional crisis or protecting herself symbolically by the only method she feels works for her. You do not have the complete picture. To change your negative judgment, all you have to do is say one of the words, such as "cancel," and switch your thinking to something like the following: "It's interesting how we all choose different experiences in order to learn and grow." You can be very creative in originating your own ideas.

You will find that eventually you "catch yourself" making the judgment halfway through the act. When your consciousness has expanded to a greater height, you will become aware of even the slightest impulse of a possibility of your making a judgment. When you become enlightened in this area, the tendency will be non-existent, and you will see in others only the positive.

Acceptance is the key. You may never choose another's "way of being in this world" as your own, but you must allow them to be who and what they are and on whatever level they choose to exist—free of your judgment.

When you master acceptance over judgment, you move to higher levels of conscious and unconscious awareness, and there are other practical benefits as well. Think of the hours you now have available to you that were once taken up with the time-consuming process of criticizing, evaluating, "gossiping about," and in any way judging others.

Releasing judgment in favor of acceptance is a very empowering and freeing experience. An even greater opportunity for evolution is dealing with "Self-Judgment," the next topic.

# Self-Judgment

*for Life*

**A**LTHOUGH JUDGMENT OF others is a negative exercise, judgment of self can be totally self-destructive. Perhaps early in your life or in the lives of people you know, a feeling of unworthiness was adopted. You can only be criticized, ignored, and in any way mistreated by others just so long before you begin to have negative feelings about yourself. At a young age you have no capability to deal effectively with these sensations. What happens is that these emotions lodge themselves deep within your inner being. If not altered or released, they can magnify and intensify until they are significantly out of proportion. The outcome is a lack of self-esteem or self-confidence. An extreme situation can manifest as full-blown self-hatred or even a desire to self-destruct.

If this has been your experience, a negative self image may expand to other areas of your life, and you begin judging yourself. The cycle seems endless until you are determined to make a change.

What can be done?

※ First of all you must be aware of your inner negative feelings toward yourself.

※ You may not understand their origin if the cause occurred prior to what you are able to remember.

- You make the freewill choice that you want to accept yourself.

- Rather than focusing on the negative, look at all your positive attributes, talents, and abilities.

- Use the releasing process referred to earlier to release the negative.

- Constantly monitor your thoughts, feelings, and emotions to make necessary adjustments in order to stay focused on the positive.

You were born perfect (unless of course you chose a defect to assist you with your growth and evolution). You can recreate this state of perfection in your consciousness at all times if you desire. You can, in your mind's eye, imagine what perfection feels like and let it resonate through your entire being. Isn't it easier to accept yourself with this feeling of perfection (your birthright) radiating through you? Only you, as an adult, can allow anyone to take it away from you. Remember you are in charge and responsible for your thoughts, and you can choose to think whatever you want at any given moment. The bottom line is now that you can see things from a more mature and enlightened perspective and detach from those early incidents that caused you to judge yourself, you can choose either self-judgment or self-acceptance.

What would you gain by choosing self-judgment? You would have an excuse to stay stuck in your life. Perhaps you could justify feeling sorry for yourself or shun responsibility. These states of being may serve you in some way, but they can never give you what you truly desire. By rejecting and judging yourself, you might find that others also reject and judge you as well. You are sending out a negative vibration, and negativity is magnetized to you in return.

How about self-acceptance? Can you imagine to the full extent what this feels like?—to know that you are OK or wonderful or **EVEN PERFECT!** Everything that occurs to you is for your own growth and learning—even perceived mistakes you might have made in the past. It is really a choice to dump all your old negative opinions concerning yourself and also to renounce all past rejection or criticism by others who were merely projecting their insecurities upon you.

You can choose to be strong in your own self-acceptance and create this as a constant state of mind by making the unyielding decision to do so and to begin *right now*. You must keep your consciousness focused on yourself in the present and resist allowing yourself to dwell on or drift back to past negative events and corresponding self-judgment.

It is quite out of order to judge yourself. The natural, more effortless path requires self-acceptance. Of course you might be aware of things you may desire to improve in your life, but truly you are "perfect in the present" according to where you are on your path of growth and learning. Accept this as truth if you can, or at least be open to the possibility that it is truth.

When you find it in your heart to end self-judgment and move into a consistent state of self-acceptance, you become much lighter and freer. A very heavy, potentially self-destructive burden has been lifted. Everything you engage in takes on a different, more positive overtone as excess baggage leaves your life.

What else is different or improves? One of the fringe benefits is that it also becomes easier to refrain from judging others. Judgment loses significance or importance in your life. Accepting self makes it definitely easier to accept others as you look for the positive rather than the negative. You have greater opportunities to attract others into your life who live in the positive arena of self-acceptance. This creates an uplifting way of existing in the world. You also stop placing limitations on your abilities or worthiness to have, be, or do anything that is your heart's desire. All is open to you now that you have stopped blocking good things from occurring to you. You therefore attract only positive things, beings, and situations because that is what you radiate. Your life truly changes course and becomes magical, and your process positively affects everyone else as well. Each time an individual moves from self-judgment to self-acceptance, the world moves into a higher vibration, so ultimately you are doing a great service for mankind—just through your own healing process.

Enjoy your life free of judgment. Give it a try. If you don't feel better, happier, stronger, and freer, you can always regress back into your old "comfortable" negative self-judgment and unworthiness. It is your choice. Remember you pave the way. It would be a challenge for others to judge you even half as harshly as you are capable of judging yourself. But in accepting yourself, you attract jewels from everywhere in the Universe. The first and most significant jewel is you. Accept it!

# Self-Love for Life

**I**N THE AREA OF self-love, so few experience completion and fulfillment. Many consider self-love to have a negative connotation of conceit, arrogance, or narcissism. In actuality these aspects have nothing to do with the true nature of love and are mere aberrations which are defense mechanisms for insecurity—180 degrees opposite from true self-love.

We have already viewed self-acceptance as a result of going beyond self-judgment. Although self-acceptance has positive overtones, let us go to a higher level, now, to love of self. Self-love is not involved with the ego or related to low-level, mundane experiences. The *ego* has little involvement with the *true self*. The ego can comfortably dwell in the realm of self-conceit or arrogance or narcissism, but the true self can not. In fact, the true self doesn't even fully comprehend these personality characteristics.

The true self is pure love in all respects. It may be a challenge for you to find your true self if it is covered up or protected as a result of fear. Those who are enlightened know that there is in everyone, at a deep level of being, a perfect all-knowing presence that is pure and beautiful, perfect and blissful. Unfortunately many people rarely get even a glimpse of this true inner self because there are too many layers of protective coatings separating the outer and inner selves. How have all these layers been formed? Fear has been engendered into hearts and minds and created the impression that "you are not OK or acceptable as you truly are." This feeling can originate from parents, teachers, siblings, peers, authority figures—or anyone.

As a result you inherit the false idea that it is not acceptable to be your real self. You may even lose the sense of the love of this pure perfect inner being because you now feel unworthy. Your pain of feeling unacceptable can grow or diminish depending on the experiences you encounter in life. All too often the true self fades into the background as you are too afraid of expressing your truth from this center of being. Self-expression in the highest form decreases and may achieve extinction. What is the result? What are the symptoms or outward manifestations? You adopt a false way of being in the world. It may be called "wearing a mask." In this way, you go through life playing a role and pretending to be what you feel you need to be so that others will like and accept you. What they might like or accept, however, is a false image—not the true you. So the game self-perpetuates. It is like the person who tells a small white lie which leads to another and another until there is a full-blown exaggeration of the truth. The person is then entangled in the lie or winds up in an uncomfortable situation.

The challenge is that an imbalance has been created—a war between the true self and the projected false image or mask. When you are afraid to be your true self, you can never know if people sincerely like the real you or only your self-created image. Therefore you feel even more insecure and perhaps unloved. This may or may not be true in actuality. What you do not realize is that most adults and almost all children have the ability to "see right through you" although most would never let on. You are so caught up in perpetuating your false image that you are lost and unaware that you are "exposed." You can delude yourself only so long because the inner true self continually screams inside of you demanding to be let out of its prison. It desires expression and acknowledgment because it comprehends the perfection that it is.

This true inner self is the part you are now encouraged to recognize, acknowledge, accept, and **LOVE**. This is what is termed "self-love," and it is very separate and different from the ego or personality (including all masks). Pretense does not exist at this level—only reality. It is the part of you that knows all things—especially what is appropriate for you and your participation in the world. It does not judge but comes from a position of loving, kindness, purity, and honesty. It is real!

How do you uncover, reclaim, and revive this true inner loving self? Do you want to? Is it safe? What would you experience as a result?

- When you allow your mind, with all its attending fears, to be silent, your true inner self speaks to you. You may not hear actual words but merely be aware of an inner knowing or impression. It may be experienced as what you call "intuition."

- When you receive the impulses, information, or insight from this part of you, it is important to listen.

- If you have difficulty connecting to your true self at an inner level, all you have to do is sit quietly and ask your true self to give you a symbol to represent it. Be silent and notice the first thing that comes to mind. It may be a word, image, or impression. This is your communication with your true self. Every time you want to connect at a conscious level with your inner being, all you have to do is bring forth this symbol in your mind or consciousness. The connection is automatically made.

- You can then ask questions or request guidance and insight. This inner part never abandons you or lets you down. You can count on it.

❧   When you have had some experience communicating with your inner truth, you will want to become *one* with it because this state of being is more fulfilling and comfortable than living the lie and wearing the mask.

❧   Eventually you may choose to align your personality with your true self in order to be one unified individual, free of internal–external conflicts.

❧   The more often you allow yourself honest expression from your true inner being, the easier and more natural it will become. You will feel light and free.

The result is freedom, self-expression, self-acceptance, and eventually self-love. You will discover how well your true self serves you, and you will feel deep gratitude because it always imparts the truth. Its communication makes your life simpler, freer, and more magical. Living in complete wholeness and oneness with your real self is, in the long run, so much easier than the burden of projecting a false image.

The inner true, pure, real self is a center of love. This is the basic characteristic of "self-love." You are not asked to love a manufactured ego or personality—but rather this inner being that exists only to serve and guide you perfectly through life. You are asked to acknowledge it for what it is, but of course you always have freewill choice. You can choose the pain and frustration of hiding behind a mask and projected false image, or you can blissfully float through life surrounded by the love and truth of your real self which guides you flawlessly.

When you have the courage to allow others to see and experience the truth of who you are, you will find that those who are appropriate to be in your life will love and accept your real self. They will be drawn to you by the magnetic attraction of your true self. In addition you will be recognized and acknowledged as being "real" which also makes others feel more comfortable and safe to be their true selves in your presence. The process is extremely rewarding.

You will experience so much happiness and fulfillment as a result of being your true self at all levels that the love for your total being will continually increase. Feel in your heart what the end result of pure self-love represents. Continue this feeling flowing from your heart to every cell of your body. In this way you actually speed up the process of true self-acceptance and love. The reason you have the power to accomplish this is because love is your true natural state and the original intention for your life. Refuse to allow anyone or any negative thought or fear to disturb your love of self. It is of paramount importance to your life and growth. Love is the most essential thing there is. Only when you love yourself, can you truly demonstrate love for others.

# Praise for Life

**F**OR CENTURIES throughout history, mankind lived in varying states of fear and awe concerning all aspects of life. Nature was feared, and man felt totally helpless, praying to false idols and gods to bring the conditions for healthy crops, bodies, and life circumstances. Honor, praise, and power were given, in other words, to objects or imagined "beings" outside the self.

This whole practice rejected the idea of man's power within himself to effect change in the world. Original power within a person's being had been put aside. The self had forgotten its inner power as a result of fear and doubt. Looking outside oneself for power and good fortune alleviated some of the pressure of being held accountable. An external force could be held responsible for accumulating fortune or suffering misfortune. Blame or praise would be placed on the god or deity. Mankind felt less and less powerful and more and more out of control. The feeling of unworthiness increased. Praise of self was considered inappropriate and not even a consideration. A pattern developed in which others were praised or honored for being who and what they were, but the self remained in the shadows for the most part.

How does this apply to you and life today? Once again, it is often easier to see the worth, worthiness, or power of another person exceeding that of yourself. You may constantly shower attention on those who you consider to be in control of the forces which appear to guide your life.

It is time to return the focus to the appropriate place. It is positive to praise and honor other individuals for their accomplishments, but this must be kept in proper proportion. Be alert so as not to give too much weight to others' achievements at the expense of honoring your own. Exaggerated praise of another can be a drain of energy away from your inner being. Balance is the key.

The true ultimate praiseworthy aspect in your life is often neglected. The focus of the praise referred to is toward your innermost being, that power within that guides you perfectly. It is important to honor that inner part that knows all. When you contact that place and align with the inner power, you have all your answers and solutions at your fingertips, so to speak. This is the life force and guidance of all creation. When you are in touch with your true inner power, you return to the original intent for your existence. You are in a position of "knowing what is best for you at all times." You no longer look to others and their lives for the purpose of holding yourself up to them in comparison, and you no longer consider that they know something superior to what you know. You reclaim your right to be you, even if that means being different from the norm or what others consider appropriate for themselves.

What, then, is "appropriate praise"? Externally it is to acknowledge in others their accomplishments or way of being in the world that works well for them. For you, it is honoring yourself to be your true self at all levels. It is also important to give yourself credit and acknowledgment for all you do well. Your focus needs to be maintained inwardly and brought back from an exaggerated dissemination of power outward to external forces or beings.

You could probably write volumes about other people. Libraries and bookstores are filled with books containing biographies describing the lives, successes, and accomplishments of famous individuals. How does it make you feel when you read those books? Do you feel inadequate in comparison? Or do you feel inspired? Do you get a sense of "If they did it, so can I"?

The truth is that your basic self can do all anyone else can. The question is whether or not it is appropriate for you. Don't get so caught up in the successes of others that you lose sight of you and your unique talents and qualities. Others, whether you are conscious of it or not, are presently holding themselves up to you in comparison. As links of a chain, each looks to another as being superior in some way. Everyone has the potential to be the best he or she can be. Look to your inner momentum and power, and take the opportunity to honor yourself at the point where you are on your life's path. Realize that whatever you do is always for learning, so give credit to yourself for your continuous movement through life.

Appropriate praise is a matter of honoring your inner true self first and then noticing the reflection of this strength, beauty, and power in others and their lives. If it were not within your being, you would not recognize the positive in others. You have unique and special talents, abilities, and characteristics in perfect combination for your life's plan. Praise, honor, and feel gratitude for them rather than looking to others for confirmation or validation of who you are and the weaving of your life's tapestry. Praise be first and foremost to you.

# Belief for Life

**T**HE POWER OF BELIEF can be measured only within yourself although the outward manifestation exists for all to see. It is the inner belief that guides and propels you in various directions through life and creates your reality.

Early, in fact soon after birth, your belief system begins to be established for you. It will be there for you to work with during your lifetime. The primary molders of your belief system are your parents or primary caretakers who instill their own beliefs and prejudices into you. You have no means available to you as an innocent, trusting child to evaluate the conscious and unconscious impressions you are receiving, so up until a certain age, you accept most of what comes in and formulate your beliefs around those of your parent figures.

Some of the beliefs are transferred into your being almost through osmosis without your conscious knowledge and become lodged deep within your subconscious. You may not be aware they are present, but you can observe the results of them in your life.

The multitude and range of beliefs would be overwhelming if you could explore them in their entirety. Even the most insignificant aspect can play a role in your life's choices and decision making. You may have gotten the idea that certain people are acceptable or unacceptable depending on their status or physical appearance. You may believe that money is the "root of all evil." You may believe it is inappropriate to do certain things on certain days of the week or to eat certain foods. The list is endless.

What really happens as a result of your beliefs, known or unknown to you, is that they affect and often control the majority of your choices and decisions throughout your life. Sometimes this is positive and advantageous. Other times it can be negative, causing restrictions, limitations, or problem issues.

Some of the manifestations that can occur are interesting and amazing. One of the greatest concerns today is the challenging issue of weight control. Books, magazines, newspapers, radio, and television constantly reinforce the belief that you must be slender and fit to be acceptable in society. This first becomes ingrained on an individual basis and then expanded to a societal belief. What happens as a result is that people actually "believe" they are not acceptable if they do not match society's ideal body image. They also accept the latest (and possibly contradictory) information that certain foods, exercise, heredity, and who knows what else governs their bodies. You may find value in some of the information; however, it is what you "believe" concerning your own body that in reality controls its shape and size. Those who truly believe they can't gain weight actually can not. Those who believe they will always have a weight problem always will. It is true that heredity, exercise, diet, and many other factors are significant, but the "belief" of how one's body "is" plays the major role. External physical change will not be permanent until the belief is entrenched at a deep level.

Some beliefs are extremely useful in assisting you through life. What do you suppose would occur if you were programmed with the belief that "everything you do comes easily," or "all you touch turns to gold," or that "whatever you attempt results in instant success"?

Whatever you believe manifests in your life. If you don't know what your particular beliefs are, how can you find out? You can use the process of reversal. This is how it works:

> Take an overview of your life. Examine your relationships, body, career, financial status, your home environment—any aspect or situation of your life. Be honest and objective as to how you view it.

> Describe your impressions of each of these separate areas, (you might want to take notes).

> What you see or interpret is what your true belief is. On a deep inner level, you unconsciously create your life and circumstances according to the beliefs you hold.

You might deny this at a conscious level by saying, "No way would I ever create that negative aspect in my life." However, you might easily be able to see how you create the positive in your life through your positive beliefs. Denying the negative is merely an escape from the challenge of taking responsibility.

You *are* responsible for the results of your beliefs as soon as you recognize that they exist. Stand back and observe. Do this without judgment. You acquired these beliefs, positive or negative, to assist you to learn, grow, and evolve.

Now if you have discovered that you have beliefs that you are dissatisfied with and would like to alter or eliminate, how do you do so?

> Observe with honest awareness and admit that the beliefs belong to you.

> Decide what beliefs you choose to keep and which you desire to let go.

> If you were free of certain old, negative beliefs, what new ones would you like to acquire to replace them? Make the

decisions from your heart. This is an important step because it will determine the future course of your life. Take some time with your choices.

❧ Once you have decided what beliefs you now desire, create the exact wording to describe them. Choose your words carefully. Be sure to use only *positive* wording. Repeat this new belief often with much positive feeling. Feel the new belief becoming a part of you in every cell of your body. Reject any doubts because doubt is what can self-sabotage you at this point. Constantly monitor your thoughts and feelings to assure that your new desired beliefs are being reinforced.

❧ It might be beneficial to work on a single belief at a time until you perfect this process.

How will you know when your newly desired beliefs have become part of you, fully incorporated? Once again use the reverse process and honestly look at all aspects of your life. When you notice positive changes, realize that the only way they could have occurred is for your beliefs relating to them to have first changed. What about luck or miracles? Yes, these do occur and can positively affect change in your life. However, you must have the belief system that can accept, be open, and even expect them to occur.

Your beliefs are in your hands. The more you realize that you are responsible for what you *now* believe, the easier it will be to make changes in your life. You can read thousands of books and attend classes day and night in attempt to improve yourself, but the only way to truly permanently effect positive change is to change your beliefs. Whatever you choose is your own free will and for your learning experience. You may accomplish all on your own timetable. Your beliefs will change when and if you are ready. It is your choice as to how much pain and suffering you want to endure as a result of your negative beliefs. It is also your choice how much happiness, success, and fulfillment you want to create by adopting and claiming positive beliefs and fully incorporating them into your life. Believe that this is truth.

# Peace for Life

**T**HERE HAS BEEN MUCH concern, desire, and talk surrounding the issue of world peace. It is uncertain, however, what that would signify for each individual life. If all countries united as a whole with the goal of peace, what would really be different in each personal experience? The world is truly a reflection of what the collective consciousness thinks and believes, and each individual in turn benefits or suffers according to whether the vibration is positive or negative. The positive vibration must supersede the negative for peace to occur on a world-wide scale. Balance is necessary in the duration of the shift from the negative orchestrating mentality to the positive thrust of peace. World peace cannot occur overnight because the shift of energy would be too great. The process needs to be gradual so all can stay in balance.

An individual's life is parallel to the larger totality of states and nations. If people in individual families cannot agree on simple issues, how can separate foreign countries expect to co-exist peacefully?

Where does it all begin, and what is your role? Peace does not begin "out there" somewhere. You might have heard the saying, "Peace begins at home," or "Peace begins in the minds and hearts of men." What does this really mean, and what is the message for you? These words hold great truth.

You have probably heard of the theory concerning microcosm and macrocosm. That is what is being related here in a sense. What you think and feel on an individual level transfers to the larger realms of city, state, nation, and world. Yes, you individually and collectively are responsible for the creation or destruction of peace. It begins with a thought or emotion and transfers, intensifies, and magnifies outward at great speed to affect all that exists.

Great scientists have stated that everything in existence is energy—in motion or vibration. New science, especially physics, deals extensively with this phenomenon. Thoughts and feelings are also energy in motion. They begin uniquely in each individual being and move outward to affect everyone and everything. This originates the creation or destruction of peace.

When you feel or think peaceful thoughts or emotions of love, joy, happiness, and bliss, on an energy level you feel at peace. Those around you feel your positive serene energy and are affected by it as well. They may feel calmer or more peaceful just by being in the presence of the energy you are radiating. Inversely, if you are feeling fear or anger, others will absorb this vibration from you and be negatively influenced.

Are you beginning to comprehend your sense of responsibility here? It's like the "snowball effect" in the culmination of energy. All the people you have affected or influenced by your state of being (peace or unrest) in turn impress all those individuals close to them with the same energy—and on, and on, and on.

Entire systems and structures of countries eventually are affected, from small community gatherings to large governmental bodies. If you ever believed that you as "one person" were helpless to cause change in the world, this was in error. Each thought or feeling you have at any moment has an effect on all that exists. You are uniquely responsible for your own peace of mind and also the overall global peace or state of conflict between countries.

It is probably easier to conceive of how your own thoughts and feelings affect your personal peace and harmony within your individualized life and family. You may have noticed that when one member of a family is in a bad mood, it can become contagious. Soon the other family members begin responding in like fashion. Subsequently their friends and their friends' families may unconsciously pass it on.

What can you do to prevent the spreading of negative energy in order to retain a peaceful state of mind and ultimately assist the world?

꧁ *Be aware* when you feel an emotion or think a thought that is less than peaceful. You cannot prevent the thoughts and emotions. It is what you do with them that is important.

꧁ Comprehending how this thought or feeling adversely affects you and other human beings as well as world peace, you realize that at this very moment you can change or "shift" the energy from negative to positive just by deciding to do so. You may think, "So and so or such and such really makes me angry, and I am going to react by retaliating"—a typical angry response. The alternative is to choose a peaceful response, "So and so or such and such really makes me angry. However, I choose to live in a state of serenity for the greater good and benefit to me and all others. Consequently, I release my emotion of anger and replace it with a feeling of non-judgmental acceptance."

꧁ At this point the transfer of negative energy is diffused. It is neutralized, and the spreading of conflict is terminated. A beneficial service to humanity had been accomplished.

꧁ When you are vulnerable to being affected by the negative energy of someone around you who has no conscious awareness of what they are perpetuating, you can participate in the cessation of their negativity. You can create your own protection and not allow yourself to be affected. Imagine the negative energy radiating out from the negative person like a wave. Also imagine you have a protective shield encircling you so that "their waves" cannot get close to you or affect your energy. You, by doing so, have maintained your tranquil state of mind as well as having made a contribution to world peace.

Each individual energy raising process of this nature is much greater in concept than you can imagine. Every thought, feeling, and response you allow to exist within you and radiate out to others creates personal as well as global peace or disharmony. You can choose to participate in the creation of world peace. By disseminating peace and love from within you out to others, who subsequently radiate this positive energy to even more people, the world as a whole becomes more peaceful. You are honored, acknowledged, and thanked each time you choose this course of action.

Peace be with you!

# Charity for Life

**T**HE CONCEPT OF CHARITY has become popularized today. There are thousands of organizations and individuals devoted to serving others through their involvement in "charitable" pursuits. Numerous individuals develop or create causes in which to engage themselves and quite often exhibit much emotional intensity concerning those causes. The individuals that volunteer their time and energy are to be commended for their caring, dedication, and concern for others.

What is the reason for including this topic? You have most likely heard the saying, "Charity begins at home." There is much truth to this statement although it may not necessarily be understood. Consider a family in which the mother or perhaps the father becomes so wrapped up in doing for others in the form of community or charity work that the family feels ignored or that they're not having their individual needs met. Family members at home have a challenge understanding why they take second place. When this occurs, the family is in jeopardy. Focus, attention, and priorities have expanded externally at the expense of internal family needs.

What are the ramifications, and how can they be resolved? So many in today's society are needy. If you are involved in volunteer or charity work, what needs to occur, even prior to caring for your family, is to practice "charity towards yourself." What does this mean? Many of the well-intentioned individuals involved in charity work ironically have unconsciously gotten into volunteering to avoid completing their own personal journey. Charity work may have become an escape from dealing with personal and family issues. Honest self-observation is required because usually this motivation is totally unconscious. Who stops to question the true motives for performing charity work? It is considered an appropriate, unselfish gift of time and service. Rarely are you criticized for your desire to assist others.

But have you helped yourself first? By completing your own personal process and becoming clear about who you are and your true purpose, you even better serve others. You must serve yourself first. If you do so, you will be a more complete and fulfilled individual and have more to offer in your service. It is time to stop putting yourself at the end of the line. How many of you have said, "After this project is completed, I am going to take time for myself"? This attitude may *appear* to be the appropriate one because self-sacrifice is reinforced by society. Is serving yourself and attending to your own personal needs and process *first* being selfish? Quite the contrary! Those who fulfill their needs prior to venturing out into the community to serve present themselves as more whole individuals and stronger role models.

When your own personal needs are met, you can assist others without underlying distractions. You are free from feeling torn or in sacrifice, or that there is never time for you. Many, many people experience this frustration without understanding it or being aware of the cause and the importance of effectively dealing with it.

The danger is that so many individuals engaged in external charitable pursuits prior to completing their own personal commitment to themselves eventually become extremely out of balance. The external activities provide an excuse to avoid working on yourself (which may be more challenging than any outer work you could find).

Charity truly begins with you being charitable and in balance and harmony with yourself. Fulfill your own needs before immersing yourself in the needs of the world, and all will profit to a greater extent. This is **NOT** being selfish! It is being true to yourself and your need to be whole. A whole, complete individual functions at a superior level than one who is fragmented, scattered, and out of balance in his or her personal life.

How can you remain balanced in regard to charity?

- When the opportunity to engage in a charitable organization or event presents itself, take time to clearly observe all that is involved.

- Ask yourself if you can devote the required number of hours and still have sufficient time for the other things that are important to you. Have you completed the things essential for your own personal growth and evolution that make you feel whole and complete as an individual, or are you looking for an excuse to put them on the back burner?

- Be honest about exploring your true motivation. How will the project or organization serve you? Are you engaging in the activity to make yourself feel good? Are you looking for recognition? Do you feel guilty because you think you are more privileged than others?

- Observe what is really most important to you. If the volunteer opportunity had not presented itself, how would you spend your time?

- Do you feel basically complete and whole and fulfilled within yourself (although of course there may still be things you would like to do or experience)?

- Are you able to balance self with outside charity work, or do you lose yourself in the process?

These questions represent a partial list of the considerations you may focus on when deciding how to allocate your time and attention. Serving others is important, but remember that your first responsibility is to yourself and to being all you can be. Then serve others in perfect balance and harmony. The more complete and in balance you are with your life, the greater your gift. Take time to observe without judgment how you have conducted your life so far. Have you used service to others as a means to escape serving yourself or taking responsibility for your life first? There is no judgment here—only your own path of learning and growth. Where are you on this path? Are you serving yourself and others in proper proportion and balance? The choice is yours.

# Hope vs. Self-Determination

**H**OW MANY TIMES have you said or heard some-one say, "I hope _____ "? What does this sig-nify? What occurs at the "other end" of a hopeful thought?

Hope is a word that is best used sparingly because it symbol-izes a sense of powerlessness. Every time you use the term, you are indicating that you have no control over the future. In rela-tion to others and their lives, this is true, and it is only appro-priate to desire the "best" or "most positive" outcome for them, whatever that is. This is one way of spreading good will to humanity, and it is an appropriate way to disseminate positive energy.

When you express hopeful thoughts, however, for your own future (where the outcomes of hope lie), you are removing your-self from the power of the present. Yes, *hope* is future-oriented. How many people feel they can create or determine their future which seems so nebulous? Why is it that when you express "hope," there is almost a subtle underlying nuance of "fear"—indicating that there is equal possibility that the object of hope is "far out there" or quite possibly unattainable.

Who or what is responsible for creating "hoped for" desires or results? Some unknown force? Maybe. Do you have a role in determining the outcomes?

You have a greater role than you might imagine. Whatever happens in your mind, heart, thoughts, and speech today determines the outcome of your future. Here enters "responsibility." If you want to know what lies in your future, all you need to do is look at the thoughts you are thinking and listen to the words you are expressing today. This is how future events are created.

Has anything ever happened in your life that you later realize is what you "feared" would happen? Have you ever been afraid of losing a job, relationship, or money and subsequently that is exactly what resulted? Has any event come to pass that occurred exactly as you thought it would? Look back for a moment. Have you ever felt something strongly and then experienced it appearing in reality? This is called self-determination, also referred to as manifestation. This process is a very important aspect of your life because the millions of thoughts that run constantly through your mind all play a role in determining your future. Since all impressions are balanced and totaled, you may want to make certain your thoughts are consistent with what you "hope for." If you desire a certain object or outcome and you also have "fear or doubt" in your mind that it will not come to pass, you are sending mixed messages to your inner creative power. If you do not receive what you desire or hope for, it is only because your negative doubting thoughts or mind energy have confused the creative process. Mixed messages put a "hold" on the process of creation. Comprehend that you are creating at every moment with your thoughts.

An even more powerful tool of creation or manifestation involves the words that come out of your mouth because as you speak you set a stronger energy vibration in motion which acts as a magnetic force to bring you what you verbalize. If you exhibit strong emotion with what you say, the speed with which you manifest increases significantly. Are you now understanding the extreme importance in choosing what you think and say and your intensity of doing so? This requires a great deal of expanded conscious awareness and dedication and is not mastered instantly. Being aware is the key, and then the choice is up to you.

You may say, "But I can't help what thoughts come into my mind." This is true, but it is what you do with those thoughts that matters. When positive, empowering mental images enter your mind, it is advisable to embellish, reinforce, and even verbalize them with emotion. On the other hand, when negative thoughts find their way into your mind, you can dispel their creative force in your life by rejecting, canceling, or erasing them from your consciousness. Do so as soon as you are aware of them. You might want to say out loud, *"erase, cancel,"* or a word that means the same to you.

After you cancel out the negative thought which is creative energy in motion planting a seed, dig up this seed and replant a new one, or positive thought. Decide how you want to transform the previous thought, being especially quick to transform thoughts of fear concerning the future.

This process is important to complete for feelings and emotions as well because they possess an "added charge" to accelerate the manifestation. You do have choice and the power to alter your thoughts, words, and emotions at every given moment. Is it now clear how you can determine your future by the thoughts, words, and emotions you are engaged in at present? Your future lies with you—not in the nebulous formless image of something you "hoped for." You are in control. If you hope for something, be aware of your role in determining if you will reach your objective.

Previously there was discussion of hope in relation to other people. You take on great responsibility if you engage in hoping to change the course of life, events, or experiences of another person. The thoughts or desires you express for another are projected to them and have a definite creative force. If you are going to engage in "hoping" for others, it is imperative you truly know exactly what they desire. This can be complicated because sometimes people do not express what they truly want. They may say one thing and deep down desire something opposite or different. There is no way you can accurately obtain this information about another individual. It is totally out of order for you to make a judgment or evaluation on your own concerning what a person needs and then to hope for that to occur for them. No matter how well-meaning your intentions, this is a great violation and infringement of their self-determination. You cannot know the path they have chosen at soul level or the experiences they require for growth. The only time it is appropriate to engage in wishing, desiring, or hoping for another is when asked specifically by that individual to do so. When and if this occurs, ask them precisely what they want you to envision for them. Remember, it is totally inappropriate and out of order to clean up other people's "stuff."

If you ask others for assistance in your creative process, be very sure you express to them *exactly* what it is you desire. The greatest reward, however, results from your own self-determination.

It is time to be consciously aware of your power to self-determine your life and future. The power lies in your present state of consciousness and actions, not in the formless uncertainty of hope. Allow hope to plant the seed, and then you pick up the watering can of responsibility and self-determination. Purify your intentions and set the conditions. The result tomorrow is what you determine today.

# Honesty for Life

**O**NE OF THE MOST highly revered virtues over the course of time has been *honesty*. It is of prime importance to "tell the truth." But how can you tell the truth when you have been engaged in successfully blocking it from yourself? Even if you do know the truth, is it safe to speak it?

Throughout history, many have died in the pursuit of and expression of truth; however, in today's society, telling "little white lies" to make someone else feel better is often considered acceptable. Reaching for truth of being and expression in your life is a goal well worth pursuing. How do you achieve a life of truth and honesty?

It is first and foremost important to be honest with yourself. This can be a considerable challenge because denial has become an habitual way to escape or avoid honesty within yourself. Denial is a type of escape mechanism that goes on automatic whenever you don't wish to or are afraid to look at the truth.

Some of the most challenging aspects to be honest about are your true feelings—to the point that you mask them so that, hopefully, others won't uncover them. Masking protects you from feeling threatened or vulnerable. When you hide your feelings to the outside world, you feel superficially safe; however, there is a downside to this experience. When you do not allow expression of your true feelings, they are retained, suppressed, buried, or denied within you. In addition, continuously striving to present a false image or "front" requires considerable energy and effort.

When feelings are suppressed or repressed, they ultimately demand an outlet. The physical and emotional bodies cannot tolerate a lifetime of hidden emotions locked within. They are similar to an erupting volcano—desiring to be free to come to the surface. Inappropriate emotional outbursts, totally out of proportion, could result. There is a greater danger that the culmination of denied expression of true feelings can result in serious emotional or physical disease. The immune system of the physical body is adversely affected by the stress of unexpressed emotions.

How do you progress to the condition of health-threatening situations without realizing what is occurring? As small children you may have been taught that "it is not acceptable to be who you truly are" or to express yourself naturally and freely. Children are frequently rewarded for behavior deemed polite, "grown up," or regarded as appropriate by adults. Because they are punished for behavior contrary to that imposed on them by parents or caretakers, they learn at an early age to play the role or game of life that makes them feel most secure. This role or false image is often contrary to their true feelings. They are forced to contain outbursts of feeling and expression of anything considered disagreeable to adults. Is it any wonder why children go through a rebellious stage? This is one avenue for them to seek emotional salvation. It is a way of rescuing honest self-expression. Ironically, however, this rebellious form of self-expression is not totally honest because it is typically carried out according to the guidelines of the peer group.

Later on in life when searching for a relationship or life's companion, you again may be tempted to present a false image of who you really are and to take on those characteristics you feel your prospective partner wants or desires. You may be able to carry out your charade for a while, but eventually your true inner self yearns to "get out" and be accepted for who it is. Yet it fears rejection if it expresses honestly.

A parallel situation exists in almost any reference point of life, from the frustrations of childhood to the challenges of adulthood, living and dealing with all aspects of society. Is it actually OK to be and express who you are and to be honest about your true feelings, thoughts, and beliefs? Yes! In fact it is absolutely essential for health and happiness. Honest self-expression is one of life's great lessons.

Perhaps adults will one day accept the honest expression of children without severely limiting their well-being. Until that time, focus is on assisting those adults who are already impaired to now learn honest expression. This is a process of "undoing" and then stimulating growth toward wholeness. You may never totally be able to express your complete truth to the outside world. It may not even be healthy or desirable to do so. What is of essence is to be totally honest with yourself. It is "OK" and acceptable to feel any way you do. There is always a valid reason for your true feelings. Once you allow yourself to honestly look at them as they present themselves, you can then decide whether or not you choose to express them outwardly. Be assured that it is natural to have them.

If emotions have been bottled up inside you, they may have become exaggerated or distorted out of proportion over time. When you make the commitment to bring them up and observe them, you are ready to deal with them. You may want to change, alter, or release those that no longer work for you.

How can you determine if you have suppressed or been dishonest with the acknowledgment or expression of your true feelings? If you are totally open and honest with yourself and are capable of expressing honestly when you desire to do so, you have greater control over your life. Balance, harmony, and self-acceptance through understanding emerge and become characteristic of your life. If you have been wearing a mask or playing the role of deception, you most likely experience considerable stress in your life.

* To become aware of suppressed or repressed feelings, thoughts, or behavior, tune into the sensations of comfort or discomfort in your physical body. Ask yourself questions such as "Is this the way I truly feel or am I deceiving or protecting myself?" "Am I attempting to please others at the expense of myself?" Realize that protecting yourself by denial of your true self is short lived and ultimately destructive.

* After observing, **BE HONEST WITH YOURSELF!**

* As long as you observe your true thoughts, feelings, and emotions with total honesty and acceptance, you are able to stay in balance.

* Now that your truth is no longer buried within your inner being in a state of denial or repression, it is your choice whether or not to verbalize it to others.

* You can express or release according to what feels most honest to you.

You gain greater self-appreciation and self-validation every time you honestly acknowledge and accept your truth of being. When you are in balance, the choice of expressing your truth is up to you. To facilitate the healing of others, you can show appreciation when they trust you with their honest expression. Children can be helped considerably by being allowed their free expression and given your acceptance. When allowed to be themselves, youngsters can grow into healthy, balanced adults.

When you decide to assume the expression of honesty, be gentle with yourself and proceed at a speed that is comfortable for you. You do not have to bare your soul to the world. Honesty with yourself is what is important. Your expression to others is your choice. Being true to yourself empowers you and sets you free.

# Truth for Life

**T**RUTH ABIDES IN YOU at the innermost core of your being. You have your own individualized personal truth that is unique to you. In other words, what is true for you may not be true for someone else. Your truth is determined by your belief system, values, experience, environment, lessons to learn, and purpose in life. The important knowledge to be aware of is that you store your own personal truth within.

What does "living in your truth" really mean? It does **NOT** mean living according to someone else's truth. In the early formative years, most children are guided by parents' or primary caretakers' philosophies. You may temporarily or permanently have adopted some of your parents' beliefs as your own. Sooner or later, however, you may begin to question some of the concepts you have been taught. They may not feel comfortable to you. If this occurs, accept the possibility that they do not represent *your* truth. They may be perfect for those who taught you (no judgment) but not for you.

Whatever does not work for you (or what feels uncomfortable) is *not* your truth, so you might want to consider dumping it as soon as possible. Rid yourself of the excess baggage so you can be free.

As essential as it is to dump old baggage or someone else's baggage that does not work personally and positively for you, it is equally important to establish your own truth. When you hear, read, or become aware of something that rings a bell with you and feels "right" or comfortable, you may respond to it as, "Yes, I believe that" or "I feel that's true." The positive reaction sets up a resonating force or vibration which is in harmony with your belief system, and this then becomes your truth. You may have heard people say, "I resonate well with that" when they hear something to which they react favorably.

What is your truth is *your truth*. It may not be appropriate for anyone else in your hemisphere of influence—even your family, so it is never advisable to attempt to impose your truth or beliefs on another. Each must establish his or her own truth independently. Interference and infringement are **OUT OF ORDER**.

What if something you believed in the past to be true for you all of a sudden doesn't feel right anymore? Allow the change to occur. Truth changes, and what might have been appropriate ten years ago or even two days ago might not be appropriate today. You need to monitor your feelings in order to stay abreast of your truth and retain balance and harmony in your life.

What happens when you are not living in your truth, or accept someone else's truth against your better instincts? In a sense you lose touch with who you truly are. There are advantages of learning from others and copying some of their process in order to obtain desired results similar to what they have achieved. However, this does not mean fully adopting their truth at an inner core level. Modeling others is a superficial or surface process that serves you only temporarily to achieve a goal. When you falsely adopt someone else's truth, you feel out of control. You cannot live someone else's life, and it may feel like that is what you are attempting to do. Soon you may lose touch with what you truly believe and feel lost or trapped.

What is required to set yourself free is to once again find the real you. Ask yourself the vital questions, "Is this true for me, or am I following someone else's truth blindly or unconsciously?" When you ask these questions you will obtain a sense of what is true for you. Use your physical and emotional bodily sensations to assist you to determine your truth. Comfort is truth, discomfort is not. Truth feels light and free. Non-truth feels heavy and restrictive.

A great challenge and, at the same time, opportunity for discovering your truth and living by it accompanies close relationships between "life partners." When you are in a close living arrangement, countless situations which could cause you to accept the truth of the other individual present themselves. You and/or your partner might be tempted to impose personal truth and will upon each other. This frequently occurs on an unconscious level for both partners. You may be attempting to control or mold your partner according to your own expectations, or perhaps for the purpose of creating more harmony between the two of you. The goal is to allow your partner to live in his or her own truth *at all times* and also for you to live in your own truth *at all times*. Be cautiously aware that there can be a tendency to influence the other innocently and unconsciously.

The recommended and positive course of action is to be constantly aware and diligently check out your truth. It has been said that "the truth will set you free." Numerous individuals have spent entire lifetimes searching for truth. They search and search, travel the world, read books, and attend classes and lectures. The discovery mission continues in the quest for the ultimate truth. Various teachings and universal truths may be uncovered along the way, and yet each person is convinced there is a greater truth lying "out there" somewhere. The search can continue for years and even lifetimes without satisfaction. The reason is because truth does not exist in a place external to you. Your only meaningful and real truth lies within you. Find it within yourself first, and then you can observe it in the outer world.

There are treasures for you to discover in the exploration of your own truth which may be ever changing. This is not an area in which you can be given a step-by-step curriculum because your exploration will be unique to you. When you see the light and live your truth, you are free.

# Independence

HAT GREATER GIFT could you possess in the process of living your life than to be happy, free, and independent? This was the original intent for everyone. How many people would describe their life situations as such? In today's society so many individuals have adopted dependencies on people or things outside themselves that they have lost the sense of what being independent truly is. An entire study and curriculum on co-dependency exists today.

When you think of an "independent individual," what comes to mind? Do you think of someone overly strong and powerful or perhaps a recluse with little human contact? Most people are unconscious of the original intent that they "be" independent. Due to a loss of confidence in self, a dependence on others develops.

Obviously, it is appropriate that small babies depend on grown-ups for their nurturing and sustenance. They have no available means to them for self-sufficiency. When you are a toddler, you exhibit your first desires for becoming independent. As a small child you may have demanded, "Let me do it myself." When allowed to "do it yourself," a feeling of capability, confidence, and independence occurred. When the primary caretakers allow children this positive expression during the formative years, the entire lives of those children evolve more into the "independent" realm as a result. The reason is that their subconscious minds accept the idea that they "can do it themselves," and a positive independent mind-set is established and placed into motion. This mind-set continues unless a greater, more dramatic, or traumatic situation occurs to offset the original intent.

What occurs with the child who is not allowed independent self-expression—the one who always has everything done for him or her because the parents lack an awareness of the importance of establishing independence? This child adopts feelings of insecurity and a lack of self-confidence which can continue through life unless a major shift appears to create that important sense of independence. A shift sometimes occurs if a situation causes children to fend for themselves out of necessity.

How, then, are childhood experiences reflected in an individual's adult life? What are the characteristics of independent people versus dependent ones?

Healthy, independent individuals may have many acquaintances and relationships but rely on themselves to motivate through life. Associations with others are by preference and choice rather than necessity. These people do not need to ask opinions or advice from others because they are accustomed to making choices independently. They feel secure in the awareness that they know what is appropriate for themselves.

Dependent individuals, however, may go from person to person asking advice and opinions on a majority of their personal life's choices and decisions. Most likely they will receive a multitude of conflicting opinions which creates even greater confusion.

You have probably heard the term "independent thinker." Few achieve this state of being because they are continuously challenged by others, along with their own self-doubts. What is required again is to trust yourself. When you are overwhelmed with decisions, it may seem more expedient to ask another's opinion which falsely lifts the full burden of responsibility off you as the decision maker. It appears perhaps advantageous to have input from various sources prior to making a decision, and it may be on occasions. Stay conscious and aware.

There are experts, specialists, and consultants who have chosen the vocation of providing advice or consultations, and when viewed as "educational," this is positive. Decisions, however, must not be left up to the expert advisor but be made independently according to the array of available information. Interestingly enough, after a person has consulted all obtainable knowledge and advice, the final resolution is often identical to the decision maker's original intuitive feeling concerning the outcome. Was all the uncertainty and investigation necessary? Everything is a learning experience.

Most people have lost their original ability to make confident independent decisions based upon their intuitive feelings. The intuitive process, however, is a major key to independence. The more often you follow your inner knowing, the more consistent the positive results in your life. The more you listen to others and follow their advice at the expense of your inner knowing because you think they "know better" than you, the greater the chance of an incorrect or inappropriate choice and resulting negative outcome.

What about people who feel stuck in their lives, unable to move forward because they depend on another to make all their life's decisions? This can occur in marriages and even in some situations involving grown children with dominating or over-controlling parents. Once the pattern is established, it is a challenge to break free, and a major event may need to occur to jar the dependent people out of their rut and catapult them into independence. Many may continuously and perhaps unconsciously choose to go through life under the thumb of another who plays a major role in making all their decisions.

It may also be stated that many individuals seek out co-dependent relationships in attempt to resolve their own issues. They project their own self-responsibility onto others who are happy to accept it.

How can true independence be realized and achieved? To become a healthy, independent individual you may wish to experiment with the following ideas and see what occurs in your life.

🦋 First observe what pattern occurs when you have a decision to make. Do you have an initial intuitive impulse that feels right to you? Do you follow through with it, or do you begin questioning, doubting, and asking others' opinions and advice?

🦋 Look *without judgment* at the process you choose.

🦋 Disengage from your involvement (in your mind's eye) and observe the situation with detachment as though "other" characters or actors were playing your role. You can learn a lot through this method because you are free from emotional involvement.

🦋 Do you discover that ultimately your original impulse was your appropriate decision or course of action?

🦋 If you feel that "others" know what is best for you, you need to come in closer touch with your intuitive alignment because it has become distorted or blurred through being ignored or rejected. Listen and follow your intuitive knowing!

When you expand your consciousness and become more fully aware, you will realize that **YOU** truly do know what is best. When you consistently are able to follow your inner knowing into decision making and actions, you have taken responsibility for yourself and control of your life. You then also have the resulting joy of being independent and free from the constrictions and value judgments others may attempt to place upon you. This is known as "being your own person," and the effort of the learning and growth process is well worth your time and energy. The more independence you gain, the better able you are to provide a role model for others, empowering them to take responsibility for their own lives in order to achieve freedom and independence. Begin with your children or anyone who depends on you at present. Assist them to their highest potential through independent living via support and encouragement rather than domination. Functioning as a free, independent individual enables you to retain your power in cooperation and harmony with others.

# Trust for Life

**T**RUSTING IS ONE of the most challenging aspects to master because it involves belief in the unseen or unknown. We all arrive in this world with an innate tendency to trust those responsible for governing our nurturing environment. Babies can lose this precious sense of trust and become fearful at a very tender age when either expectations are not fulfilled or the "mother figure" is out of sight for an uncomfortable period of time. Trust can also vanish as early as the birthing process or immediately following when the infant is poked and inoculated in hospital nurseries.

An entire series of events follows to challenge and threaten a child's inherent sense of trust. School years provide further opportunities for distrust to grow and expand. Promises are made and then broken. Lies are told. Friends betray. The message transmitted and accepted is "I can't count on anyone for sure."

It is true that the personalities of other human beings can misrepresent things and betray your trust, but this is part of the growth and learning process. The lesson is that first and foremost you need to trust and believe in yourself. There is a force in nature and the Universe that always supports you. It exists inside of you and all around you. When you tap into this power and make it part of your reality, you are once again able to trust.

A willingness to go forward in life with a certain degree of courage is also required. You might think, "But how can I trust nature when I see evidence of all the damage and destruction that can result from natural forces?" In truth, all of what you see **IS** done for a reason and balances the natural forces on the planet. You cannot understand the causes because you do not have access to the entire picture, and you see only the destructive aspect because the creative force is often invisible. Trusting in the unseen is the challenge.

The future as well is unseen. How can you trust in the future when you have so much fear surrounding it? Fear is counterproductive to trust and represents a significantly destructive force in your life. Trusting and believing that your future will be perfect and positive is what creates it to be that way to a large degree. What you trust and believe in your heart and innermost being is what manifests in your future.

If you cannot feel trust toward others and are not sure how you feel about nature and your environment, where do you begin? The answer is simple but not so easily implemented. You must trust yourself *first*. How are you going to do this, especially if you have a group of people surrounding you who may not trust you due to their own fear? How do you receive the message and gain the confidence to trust yourself?

There is an energy within you that has all your answers and guides you perfectly once you find it. Silence yourself, listen to it, and then follow its advice. This is always information you can trust. It comes from within and is linked up to all information outside of yourself as well, just as bands, waves, and particles of all energy intermingle in the Cosmos. You have access to all information in the Universe, and it is worthy of your trust because it comes in truth. It may speak to you softly or with high volume. You may have only a subtle feeling or you may feel considerable energy movement in your physical body. This powerful message and communication center is always providing you with information you can trust because it comprehends the larger picture. It sees and knows all, and you can tap into this all-encompassing sea of knowledge at any time.

Those of you who are very sensitive to feelings and impulses may obtain the information quickly as though you were in tune with or in alignment with a sixth sense. Others may need to sit quietly and silence the chatter of thoughts in order to get in touch with this inside information. Whatever the case, what you receive from this source is always true, and you can trust it.

How do you demonstrate whether or not you trust? This is determined by what you *do* with the information you obtain from the inner level. This information, though often ignored, can be trusted 100%. Its purity and perfection is far superior to what you receive externally with your obvious five senses. When you master trusting to the desired degree, you then **ACT** on the information given to you, even if it appears as only a subtle insight or "hunch." When you act, demonstrating your faith and trust, the Universe acknowledges you by giving you more and more important and valuable information. The more you act on this derived knowledge and trust it, even greater levels of information and assistance will be given to you. This process expands and accelerates to the point at which you instinctively trust what you receive at your center of truth without questioning it or looking outside yourself for answers.

At an advanced level, you will be able to confidently glide or float through your day and every experience of life without thinking about it. You may feel as though you had pushed a button to put yourself on "automatic." As you travel through life in trust, guess what else happens? Fear disappears. This may sound at first unbelievable to you, and yet that is exactly what happens. You are given all the information you need. All you need to do is listen and trust it. Since it comes from within, **TRUST YOURSELF**.

How does this relate to relationships with others? Unfortunately, you do not know which individuals are listening to their inner resources and responding according to this guidance. You cannot be sure if they are acting in their truth or out of ego if you only relate to them with your external five senses. To determine whether or not you can trust others, look inside (using your inner information source) to obtain your answer. Trust what you get from within yourself, no matter how convincing to the contrary the other individual might sound or appear.

If you are the only person in a roomful of fifty people who receives a different inner message from what all other forty-nine are expressing, it does not mean that they are correct because you are outnumbered. **YOU** feel and know what is appropriate, and that is what to trust. If it is "right for you," it is **RIGHT FOR YOU!** The day may come when human awareness evolves to the level that all people tune into their inner information source and then act as *one* in truth. That day is not here yet, so the best thing you can do in the interim is to trust yourself and learn what else you can trust through trusting yourself to know that also.

# Justice for Life

**A**LTHOUGH VARIOUS civilizations have claimed to have been founded on the concept of "justice," many have ignored the original intent and have created rules of their own for personal gain. Whenever you speak about justice, clarity is essential—justice for who? And what does justice *really* mean?

You might consider justice in relation to the legal or ruling systems of countries. The underlying intention is fairness for all individuals. Of course, this incorporates and involves the areas of judgment and evaluation.

The often spoken of desire concerning "justice for all" has been stated throughout history, but what does it really signify? What it ideally means is that each person be assured of opportunity, fair treatment, and respect in accordance with all others. It also symbolizes an ideal of equality which has become nebulous in its definition as the dichotomy in societal structures is observed. Justice is a concept that many refer to but few comprehend.

What does justice stand for in your life? What can it imply? To take a broad perspective, you must go back to the concept of free will and the inhibition of it or infringement of it by others. The interpretation of justice often becomes obscured when related to your experience. Most likely no two people would agree on what "justice" signifies in parallel situations throughout their lifetime. There are too many possible alternative ways of looking at things. Belief systems, experiences, and attitudes always enter into the picture. What is termed fitting or proper for one may be inappropriate for another.

Where does justice truly exist? In actuality it lives in the heart of each individual, although its symbols are played out in societies, structures, and relationships. How many times a week, day, or hour have you questioned what was the "right" or "just" thing to do? People respond or react as though there is only one acceptable answer to this question. In truth, there may be as many "correct" alternative options or variations as there are people because ideally, justice stems from each individual's truth. Each person possesses his or her own unique personal truth at every moment and in every situation.

The purpose of this discussion is to demonstrate that one single unalterable ideal of justice does not exist. A judge in a courtroom may hand down a verdict or decision which has great impact on many lives. It may appear "just" for one and "unjust" for another. It could even seem either "just" or "unjust" for all involved. What right does one human being have to impose his or her idea of justice on another? When did humanity lose the ability to control interactions so that it was determined appropriate for certain individuals to set themselves up as judges with power over others? The evolution of justice "systems" progressed as a result of specific individuals desiring to control others who were considered weak or derelict and to determine what was "right" for them. Is it quite possible, then, to be at the mercy of one who desires to play a role in deciding your fate?

There are definite instances and situations in which you are, unfortunately, at the mercy of others to affect and determine your well-being until your consciousness rises above it. Various institutions including governments dictate to you their interpretations and definitions of justice, and it affects your life. You are taxed, for example, according to an insensitive system that knows or cares little to nothing about your personal needs and responsibilities. An unfeeling mathematically calculated chart, graph, or scale determines what you "justly" owe. This is called "justice"! Others might be able to escape taxation through their influence, power, or craftiness, and this occurrence is accepted in the present-day justice systems of many countries. There are governments out for the personal gain of a few at the expense and sacrifice of many.

In light of all the supposed "injustice" that exists, what can you, as an individual, do to co-exist and deal with these concepts? You need to basically relate to yourself in deciding what is appropriate, first for you and your family and then for your hemisphere of influence. You can only be asked to do your best in every situation, detaching when necessary in order to stay in balance.

It is important at each threshold of decision-making to listen and "feel in your heart" your own uncontaminated personal idea of justice, including the possible results or effects. It is recommended to get yourself, your biases, and prejudices out of the way so as not to be influenced. In your mind's eye, look at each situation as though you were totally removed from it. This helps get your ego out of the picture as well. Pretend you have no personal gain in the outcome, and you will make a fair decision. There is a lot of old mindgame "stuff" that must be eliminated from everyone's consciousness. Each situation is different and needs to be looked at or observed free of past influences.

As you may now understand, you cannot control what others do or create in the name of justice. All you can do is act "justly" according to your own insight and remain clear and in the present with each event that presents itself. The only *true* justice is your own unique personal determination. You do not have to accept, as your individual idea, what another determines to be just. Be clear in your own heart about what you "know" is just. It takes a lot of awareness and detachment to live happily in a world fragmented in its concept and implementation of justice. If you allow *your* concept of justice to dwell in your heart, determining your personal responses and actions, you create balance. This is your challenge.

The more you purify your thoughts and feelings and raise your consciousness, the less unjust interference you will experience in your life.

# Self-Realization *for Life*

**H**OW OFTEN DO YOU stop to tune into and observe your life from the higher perspective of honoring your true nature? It is definitely appropriate for you to take time for this process. Individuals typically spend greater effort recognizing and acknowledging others than paying attention to or honoring who and what they **truly** are. First of all, no one is greater than you, and you have an inherent capability to complete all you are here to learn and do.

It is time to stop focusing on the accomplishments of others and holding yourself up in pale comparison. What another is here to do is not necessarily what you are here to do because each one has a different purpose. If you admire a famous actor, artist, or writer and feel inferior because you do not have the identical talent, you are not aware of your special purpose, and you are not seeing yourself in the light of who and what **YOU** truly are. You have special talents and abilities that are unique and in perfect combination for your life's purpose. You may have gifts still lying dormant within you waiting to be uncovered.

If you have avoided focusing on yourself and the uniqueness of who you truly are, now is the time to become centered. No one outside yourself can do this for you. You need to give this process serious attention if you want to have self-knowledge and self-realization.

As a first step, sit quietly and close your eyes. In your mind's eye, imagine and project yourself into a picture or image in the future without first thinking about it. Where are you, and what are you doing? The answer is significant because the inner all-knowing part of you has been called upon to provide the answer, message, or information. The disclosure could involve something you are presently unfamiliar with or a project, hobby, or mission you have been interested in but not pursued. It is important to pay close attention to messages arising from this inner level which concern your future.

Most importantly, however, you need to be aware of the "present" and listen to your inner voice for one-step-at-a-time information. When you follow each step as guided in perfect order, you will also arrive at your goal or intended purpose. You truly do not need to see and usually are not given the entire picture, and this is appropriate. The reason is that what is involved here is the challenge of trusting the process of gradual growth and evolvement. You may not understand the reason you are given a certain message at an inner level to go somewhere or do something. The direction can be as simple as to call someone on the phone when you have no apparent reason for doing so. Later on, in retrospect, you understand the connection and comprehend its significance. Perhaps the individual you called told you about something or someone that you needed to contact or to be aware of that would be instrumental in guiding you to your next step. This is how your tapestry of life is woven.

It is important not to negate or judge *any* piece of information because remember that you do not have the complete picture. Trust the information you are given by your inner being, and follow it to the best of your ability. What is of essence is to reject the doubts, fears, and negative thoughts. Your logical, analytical mind may miss the purpose or fail to understand the underlying perfect pattern or significance. Therefore it could perceive your guidance as false or a waste of time or think of all sorts of reasons for rejecting what you are inwardly guided to do. At this crucial point your pathway gets blocked, and you fail to follow through or things don't work out. Your "head" takes command, and you make the choice to trust and follow it rather than your heart or inner knower. This is where you get bogged down on your pathway to self-realization and fulfillment. Here the detour begins, and the process of being led to another opportunity or piece of information (for the purpose of once again being guided back to your path) must now be revealed with the intention you will be aware, not negate, and follow this lead.

When you *do* listen and *do* follow your inner voice, free from doubting and being thrown off course through listening to your questioning mind, you are "on path." All your life's experiences begin to weave together in perfect order. You may need to wait until you are quite a way down the road to see the perfect orchestration and sequence of events that have transpired to bring you there. This is the "Tapestry of Life."

The more frequently you trust and follow your inner voice, one step at a time, the greater the amount of information that comes to you. When you reach the point at which you "get out of your head" and resist analyzing and evaluating all your inner (and outer) messages, you will be given more guidance at an accelerated rate. Much valuable time and effort will be saved.

Imagine what it could be like to watch your life unfold like a movie with a free-flowing series of events magically creating the story. You are merely observing and not attempting to change or distort the process. You are "going with it." This can symbolize your effortless path through life as well *if you are willing to allow it*. Resist over-thinking and doubting. Experiment for a day. Let yourself flow from one activity or event to another without "struggle." You may feel as though you are a puppet and someone else is pulling your strings as you are guided from place to place or activity to activity. At the end of the day, look back and observe how smoothly your day unfolded and how much you effortlessly accomplished.

"Effortless" is the description of being directly on course or on path with your life and achieving self-realization. Whenever you make your life a challenge, it is because a part of you is not listening to the inner voice. When things do not go as you desire, it is because you have made a decision to doubt, analyze, evaluate, or resist in some manner your ideal course of action. This can lead to inner confusion and a resulting lack of trust in yourself.

The point is that you really don't have to "force" anything. Listen and follow as your inner voice perfectly guides you and your own unique tapestry of life to the appropriate people, places, and things for the unfoldment of your own self-realization. Trust it to be so.

# Expectations *for Life*

**H**OW MANY TIMES have you created expectations in your mind only to be disappointed when things did not turn out as foreseen. Expectations quite often involve another person who voices and demonstrates his or her own freewill choices. You may desire a certain outcome, but when another individual is drawn into your life, you cannot exert your will over that person's. When you create expectations surrounding another, you may be setting yourself up for disappointment. In reverse, if you do not have expectations concerning other people, you will not be distressed.

In essence, you can rely only on yourself to fulfill your expectations. By so doing you also avoid infringing on another's freewill choice. Remember that you cannot know or predict what is appropriate for someone else because in no way can you perceive their evolutionary path. In addition, they might choose to exercise their free will contrary to your desires or anticipations.

What is the appropriate state of existence then? The balanced state is one of you committing to be the best you can be at every given moment. To do so you follow your inner guidance and take total responsibility for yourself and all your life's decisions. When you release expectations of others, you free them, and you also release yourself from uncomfortable entanglements.

You can live peacefully and work in greater alliance and harmony with everybody because you do not have an investment in the outcome of their actions or decisions. Your involvement becomes one of mutual agreement and cooperation.

Your life also takes on a more relaxed attitude because you release the temptation to manipulate and control. If you have an invested interest in your relationship with other individuals, it may be a struggle or challenge to get out of their way. You may be strongly tempted to influence them and/or their lives. This is out of order and can greatly diminish your ability to stay in balance.

If expectations of others is not in order, why is self-expectation appropriate? You are ultimately responsible only for yourself, and you create your personal reality according to what you believe. If you count on doing well on an exam or project, your chances of doing so greatly increase. If you expect to lose your job or sabotage a relationship, rest assured that is the probable outcome. If you visualize others responding positively to you without attempting to control them, there's a good chance they will. If you predict rejection, that is what occurs. The explanation follows.

Expectations exist in an unconscious state as well as on a conscious level of awareness. If something occurs in your life, you can be assured that to some degree (consciously or unconsciously), you expected it or anticipated the possibility of it happening. In other words you are an "energy magnet" for what you expect either consciously or unconsciously. Observe your life honestly without judgment, and determine if what you describe is your desired result. If not, you may want to consider adjusting your consciousness.

You may be wondering about the relationship between parents and children. What is appropriate? Are parents to release expectations concerning their children and the children's behavior and decisions? Since each family and individual is unique, every situation presents its own particularity. However, a few guidelines can be offered.

Customarily it is the parents' role to teach their children the rules of the society in which they were born. This does not necessarily indicate that the rules are ideal or unalterable in the future. Parents can instruct on a range of topics such as proper etiquette and respectful treatment of others. Of course, each individual and family has its own value system although various alternatives exist throughout social systems. Most are familiar with the universal concepts of the "Golden Rule" and "You Reap as You Sow." These precepts are valuable along with societal and family rules for the growth and socialization process. Each child is presented with opportunities to experiment on both sides of a rule—to obey or to violate. The learning is in experiencing consequences. The parents' and significant adults' roles are first to present the information. The next step, once the child has a comprehension, is to silently step aside and allow the child to learn by means of his or her own personal choices and decisions. It is a tremendous challenge for adults to resist interfering at this point because they are well aware of the potential consequences and want to protect their children from negative experiences. However it is appropriate to intervene only when the child is very young, in danger, or has insufficient understanding of the situation.

Many parents cannot release their own personal expectations concerning what they want their offspring to do, be, and have because they feel their children are a symbol or reflection of themselves. What they fear is that others will judge them by their children. Unfortunately, this actually may be the tendency with "unaware" people. The optimal course of action is to detach from the judgment of others, thereby freeing yourself from being negatively affected by them. If you are guided and influenced primarily by others' expectations or opinions, you are not living in your truth. Remember that only you can know the appropriate learning and growth experiences you need.

Your ideal expectations are for you to achieve your full potential and fulfill your purpose. Other non-essential expectations can throw you out of balance and off your path. You must not judge your present position in relation to achieving your ultimate goals because you do not have the complete picture or agenda. Release inappropriate expectation, follow your inner knowing step-by-step, and you will sense a new freedom of being.

# Future Self for Life

**I** **T HAS BEEN STATED** that what you think, feel, say, and do today creates and determines what you will experience tomorrow. In reality those thoughts, feeling, words, and actions are responsible for creating your future self. Before you become aware, you might be tempted to place responsibility elsewhere. You might either condemn or give credit to your parents or other individuals for your past experiences and basis for being in the state in which you presently find yourself. A number of people are instrumental in participating in your life's experiences, but *they* are not the cause of them. The authentic cause is your own personal reaction and response to those individuals and experiences. It is the mind energy along with your thinking, feeling, and expressing processes that creates the events and results in your life.

Two people could have very similar experiences and yet create totally different realities. Children in the very same family with identical parents can live in "different worlds." What is of essence is how they think, feel about, and respond to their life experiences and interactions. What is true for one family member is not necessarily reality for another.

In a family in which the children were mistreated, one child could grow up forever fearful, never able to heal or go beyond the devastating childhood experiences. Another child might gain strength and determination from the early background and resolve to make a mark in the world or to assist others. The original event or situation is not the ultimate cause of the outcome. It is the individual's *reaction* and *response* that creates the end result.

If more people realized this truth, they might be able to choose more positive reactions and responses in order to decisively affect the consequences of their lives. This is called "taking responsibility for your life." When you arrive at this point, great personal growth occurs because you have gone beyond external blame. How do you accomplish this?

- When you are aware of something that has occurred and which leaves you feeling emotionally and negatively "charged," you most likely will have an immediate unconscious (or conscious) desire to "react" in a certain way. You may be feeling resentment, anger, or fear.

- The key is to be cognizant that your response affects your future life and future self. Remember that you have a choice as to how you respond.

- You can react impulsively, or you can take the time to reflect on how your response might affect your future.

- In your mind's eye, place yourself in the various possible future outcomes resulting from your present choice. With a little practice this becomes easy and automatic.

- Observe the results in your mind's eye, and choose the appropriate course of action and response that will bring you to the end you ultimately desire.

- Let go of the original resounding emotional charge, and discern that you have just experienced growth and witnessed creation of your future self and life in a more positive light.

There is no judgment. If you choose the impulsive response which may be negative, you will learn as well. Many choose this way of learning over and over and over again. If you are dissatisfied with the way your life appears to you at this point, reflect on your thoughts, feelings, and responses to past situations to uncover the causes.

You may not be able to modify past events; however, you can at present begin to alter your responses and transform your thinking and the future. You create a current pattern of releasing the past and initiating a new beginning. In this way you can shift the energy in a direction that will be more positive. You say to yourself, "My past response to such and such was _____. Now that I understand and perceive the effects of that response in my life, I choose to change that response (or thought, belief, or feeling) to _____."

As soon as you make the absolute decision to shift your past negative response patterns, all aspects of your life work together to generate a more positive, happy, future self. You are not at the mercy of others. You are only at the mercy of your own decisions. Once you are aware, you can then end the negative process of blaming others, which can lead only to weakness and an inability to effectively take control of your life. Other individuals and situations perfectly act as catalysts and opportunities for you to experience and gain insight.

What transpires when you stop blaming external events and people from your past and assume personal responsibility for your responses and subsequent creation of your future? You become strong, independent, light, and free. You no longer feel deprived or at the mercy of the decisions or actions on the part of others who "now" serve to provide opportunities for you to learn and respond in the most appropriate way.

How you respond determines your future self. You are capable at any moment of creating what you desire by converting former, inappropriate mind energy that held you back. The choice is yours. Freedom and security emerge from your decision to take responsibility. This is one of the greatest gifts other than love you can give yourself.

# Present Self

*for Life*

**I**T HAS ALREADY BEEN illustrated that who you presently are and the conditions of your life have been created by your past thoughts, words, and feelings. How does this process function, affect you, and maintain influence over you? The totality of your experience becomes absorbed into your physical body and remains intact at the cellular level. That is, the culmination and combination of every thought, feeling, belief, and life situation is a part of the structure and composition of every cell in your physical body.

When you alter your expressions and responses in the present moment, the cellular structure of the body changes as well. Another major area experiencing change is the brain chemistry of the body which also in turn affects every cell. All aspects work together. Thoughts of fear send a chemical which stimulates the nervous system and races through the body. Thoughts of peace and love create tranquilizing chemicals. Your emotions are very instrumental, therefore, in creating the state of health or disease in the body. Negative emotions can cause an imbalance or blockage in the healthy flow of energy. Positive emotions help keep the body healthy through the balanced and unobstructed flow of energy. Every time you have a negative emotion, the body must go through a detoxifying process just as though a chemical poison had invaded the physical body. Consequently, it is advisable to monitor your emotions at all times and release the negative ones before they can threaten your state of balance, health, and happiness. They are powerful and have a greater degree of influence on your well-being than you can imagine. Emotions affect every cell of the body. Choosing love, peace, harmony, good will, joy, bliss, and forgiveness helps you to create your life to its full potential.

What else affects your present state of being? Much has been researched and written about heredity and environment and their importance in determining who you are. However, their influence, although significant, can be overcome through the energy of the mind which is more powerful. All healing and destruction have their roots in the power of the mind. It is important to know that the mind can alter and turn around negative influences of the environment as well as inappropriate DNA information at the cellular level. Anything is possible.

When a child comes into this world, it arrives with and subsequently accepts a certain set of equipment to work with including heredity, environment, parental beliefs, and values. Then the child obtains nourishment on all levels—physical, emotional, mental, and spiritual. The nourishment can be either positive or negative. Let us consider the physical area which involves food, shelter, and clothing or bodily protection. A healthy, well-cared-for body assists the whole being to a higher level of existence. Natural, living foods promote the full potential of the body. Natural fibers in clothing are more compatible in supporting the body's temperature system. Pure water aids the electrical and cleansing systems. A clean, healthy environment with pure air serves the lungs, heart, and immune system. It is beneficial to pay attention to all you can do to assist your physical well-being.

Monitoring your emotions and reframing the negative ones to the positive have already been discussed in conjunction with thoughts, feelings, and beliefs. These processes cannot be overstressed and cannot be separated from the resulting physical condition. Another important area that affects your present self is your spiritual state of being. What is involved in spiritual well-being is at the core level of existence and relationship with self and others. Are you living in a state of unconditional love, forgiveness, letting go, and releasing, or are you holding grudges and retaining what no longer is appropriate for you? Are you listening to your inner voice for guidance, or are you following negative ego? Are you accepting, open, and committed to participating in what is for the "greater good," or are you closed and withdrawn inside yourself? There are many factors that affect the state of a healthy spirit. Living according to the integrity of your heart assures balance of spirit.

Another useful concept to adopt for a healthy state of being is to keep your major focus on the present moment. Worrying about the past or fearing the future is energy draining and deprives you of truly living and experiencing your life. The "now" is all you are assured of, and it is precious. The present is where joy and bliss dwell. Do an experiment of just "being," sensing for a few moments what you are experiencing inwardly. Feel the union with your inner being and all that exists external to you. Keep your thought processes still and just *be*. The power is in the moment. When you do this, fear disappears. You can experience the beauty, joy, love, and happiness of your true self. Still the mind as long as possible and cause your thoughts to evaporate. The more often you do this, the greater connection you will establish between all aspects of your being. You will more fully sense and understand the power of thought, feeling, and emotion over your state of existence. Silence and observation will teach you much about yourself. Take time each day in silence to know yourself. If you desire change, then work on your thoughts, feelings, beliefs, and physical and spiritual environments.

**B**LISS CAN BE VIEWED as the ultimate emotional goal. When you dwell in the state of bliss, all is perfect on all levels of being. Bliss consciousness is similar to being in an altered state because nothing is able to disturb you. You may experience a floating sensation or lightness of being. The heart area might feel expanded with either joy or calm, tranquil peace. Once you have experienced the sensation of bliss, all else pales in comparison. Bliss linked with love may be the perfect state of consciousness.

Have you ever questioned why this wonderful, happy feeling which is perfect in essence and makes you feel whole and at peace with all existence is often inaccessible? Have you ever felt overwhelming bliss and affirmed that you always wanted to maintain this incredible state of being? What was the outcome? Did you eventually backslide to lesser or even negative emotional states? If so, why?

Bliss is achieved when all aspects of yourself work together in perfect balance, harmony, and agreement. Nothing out of order exists in that moment. Unfortunately, few people are able to consistently maintain this state because a disturbance occurs at some level. You may be jarred out of bliss by someone entering your external experience with a problem or issue for you to address. You may suddenly recall something that pulls you off your peaceful cloud. Negative thinking has a way of creeping in to destroy your blissful state.

Bliss, therefore, is quite often a transient feeling which can be modified by any disruption. Once the disturbance or interruption has occurred, the feeling is diminished, and it may take quite some time to achieve it again through normal channels. In truth, however, "bliss" was intended as your natural state.

How can bliss be created and sustained? What is required to maintain this often ephemeral state is awareness and presence of mind. You need to be in touch with your feelings and also realize that you are free to choose how you want to feel at any particular moment. No one outside of yourself has the power to "make" or "coerce" you into feeling one way or another. Disruptions certainly may originate from others outside yourself, but your moment-to-moment state of mind comes from within. Observe how your unconscious responses disrupt your happiness. You may accept the saying, "that's life." Yet it shall be stated again for emphasis that at every moment you *do* truly have the choice to have control over what you feel.

When an overwhelming negative emotion crashes into your state of bliss, what occurs? Your total focus and attention move toward the negative state in order to deal with it. What choice do you have? The recommended choice of response is to stay conscious and aware of what is occurring. You may even verbalize it to yourself. "I was perfectly contented and then 'such and such' occurred to destroy my happiness." At this point you have the choice of lowering your vibration to the negative or rejecting the invasion and returning to maintaining your blissful state. How can you do this? Actually it is quite simple and seems almost too easy. You take control by emphatically stating or thinking to yourself, "I **REFUSE** to allow anyone or anything to interfere with my perfect state of bliss." As you command and order the disruption out of your mind, heart, thoughts, body, and entire energy field, you will "feel" the shift as you regain control. You are now dealing with interference at a higher level.

Another technique is to imagine a protective shield surrounding you that prevents negative disturbances from entering your energy field. Use the powerful statements, "I choose love" or "I choose happiness" or "I choose bliss." You are the creator of your life through your words, thoughts, and emotions, so it is essential to master those in order to control your life. You can do it, and it is imperative to take command. No one can do it for you. You prevail on a conscious level and choose what you desire.

Why are love, happiness, and bliss the ultimate desired states? When you live in a state of constant love, happiness, or bliss, your physical body responds by creating harmony, balance, and perfection. You are considerably less likely to become ill or diseased, and you always feel wonderful. You become an energy magnet for high vibration people who also control their own lives, and all aspects of your life improve. You attract joyous "things." Why would you want to settle for anything less than bliss in your life?

Those who choose a state of "less-than-bliss" may be doing so in order to punish themselves. They may not feel worthy of existing in a permanent state of bliss, so they sabotage their happiness by inviting in the destroyers of bliss (negative thoughts and emotions) through their own choice—conscious or unconscious. They may not be comfortable in a constant state of bliss because it is unfamiliar, and it feels strange. You are free to make whichever choice you desire. It is all a part of learning and growth. The important thing is that you are aware that you are responsible for your feelings and can consciously control them.

The more you allow yourself to continue in a state of prolonged bliss, the greater the reinforcement until you eventually can accept it as your natural intended state of being—your birthright. In the state of bliss no negativity exists, and you are unlimited. You can rise to your full potential and achieve all you desire, free of doubts and fears. Given the alternative, which do you want for your existence? The choice **IS** yours—happiness, love, and bliss or unhappiness, negativity, and fear. All is at your command and control. Either take charge of your thoughts, emotions, and life or allow it to be manipulated by external, oftentimes low-vibrational forces. If you are unconvinced, experiment creating different states of being through "allowing" and then "controlling." Discover your power to do so and rise above your old self-imposed limitations.

# Self-Confidence

**SELF-CONFIDENCE SIGNIFIES** completion of the personal challenge to believe in yourself. Why does achieving it represent such a great challenge, and why does insecurity surround so many individuals? Where does it all begin?

From the time a child first attempts to do anything for himself or herself, usually there are grown-ups present who feel the child is not ready or capable because the child's first efforts may have been less than perfect. Muscular strength and precision take time to develop fully enough for children to manipulate what they hold in their hands without dropping objects or miscalculating aim. Self-feeding can be temporarily arduous for some children, yet determination eventually obtains the desired results. During the early unsuccessful struggles resulting in failure of food reaching the mouth or in dropping a prized object, the significance of either encouragement or lack of assurance from the supervising adults cannot be over-emphasized. Do adults inspire and praise the child with phrases such as, "You can do it" or "You're doing great"? Or is the communication one of "Let me do it for you (or help you)" and "You can't do that by yourself"?

These early messages of doubt transmitted into the child's subconscious mind might appear immaterial and well-intentioned at the time; however, the perception that lodges firmly in the child's mind produces a lessening of self-confidence. The child loses faith that he or she can accomplish what is desired. Of course children must develop physically to be able to successfully accomplish certain tasks. What is important, however, is their underlying conclusions concerning their capability to achieve, succeed, and overcome obstacles. The early information relayed to the subconscious is extremely powerful and can create a dominant attitude of either confidence or insecurity.

In the classroom the children who sense their unlimited capability are more likely to excel compared to those who have integrated the notion that they are unable. The saving grace for the latter group is that the messages to the subconscious are mixed. Since they have most likely experienced successes along the way, in addition to failures, they at least have some degree of confidence in specific areas of their lives. If children learn that they can be successful in one area of life, whether it be mental ability, physical coordination, creativity, or social skills, the potential for developing self-confidence is present.

Rather than expressing criticism, fear, and concern, it would be advantageous for the surrounding influential adults to generate praise and encouragement at each minor success a child aspires to in the learning and maturing process. Since this is a simple practice, why is it so often ignored or negated? The reason is that adults unconsciously experience the reflection of their own "imagined" inabilities triggered by the unsuccessful attempts of a child. This produces discomfort and at some level reinforces their own insecurity and lack of self-confidence. They then again project doubt to the child which instills greater lack of confidence for the youngster. The pattern continues repeatedly at an unconscious level. Obviously it is not the conscious choice of adults to shatter the self-confidence of small children. They merely reconstruct the original pattern they experienced as children.

How can this cycle be terminated in order to increase confidence level and security? Awareness is the key. Be conscious that the words you utter and the manner in which you respond to others is more powerful than you can imagine—particularly in the case of a small child.

⚘ The first step is to be aware of your influence.

⚘ Make the conscious decision to be consistently encouraging, supportive, complimentary, and filled with praise.

⚘ Allow the child (and those of greater maturity as well) to do for themselves without assistance unless they ask for help.

⚘ Retain in your field of "intention," the idea that the person will succeed. Never project or anticipate failure.

It is a simple matter, once you understand the importance, to assist children to become self-reliant and self-confident. The greater challenge at hand is how to assist those adults who lack confidence and suffer from low self-esteem. How can you change the pattern if *you* feel insecure of your ability to succeed?

⚘ First you must understand that your "feeling" of insecurity is completely unrelated to the truth about your ability and that it is the result of incorrect information that has become lodged in your subconscious.

⚘ Look at all you have succeeded in accomplishing during the course of your life. Make a list and continually add to it. Include everything no matter how small or insignificant it may seem to you. Remember to add "learning to read, write, ride a bike, walk"—**EVERYTHING YOU CAN DO**. Be as detailed and complete as possible.

⚘ Magnify all your successes and talents and abilities in your mind's eye.

⚘ Look at your list often and intensify the "feeling" of success and accomplishment throughout your body. **BECOME**

**SUCCESS!** Become self-confident in creating the feeling. The more you concentrate on feeling confident, the greater the amount of self-confidence that is incorporated in the real you.

Minimize and release feelings or thoughts of ineptitude, inability, or insecurity that might surface. Replace them with positive feelings. Give yourself a pep talk and reminder of all you do well, realizing that you can successfully accomplish all you truly desire with a little determination.

Keep your focus pure, and accentuate all that is positive and successful at all times. From time to time add to your list of accomplishments.

Walk with confidence in your gait, even if you still feel a little insecure. Adopt postures and facial expressions that symbolize self-confidence.

In other words, self-confidence begins in the mind and circulates through the entire energy system of the body. Your state of being can be changed and improved at any moment by the thoughts you contemplate coordinated with your bodily actions. You become what you act out or portray.

It is essential to resist the negative influences of others. Due to the fear, jealousy, greed, and insecurity of others, they may attempt to destroy your self-confidence through criticism, judgment, and negating comments. Protect yourself from these potentially harmful individuals by first being aware of who they are and what they are attempting to do, and then by imagining a protective shield surrounding you that is repelling their negativity. As you reject the negative, accept the support, compliments, and acknowledgments from others who relate to you in a more positive way. Eventually these are the individuals you will attract into your life as your self-esteem and confidence increase. Confidence can be created at any time you choose. You can successfully complete the process with a little understanding and dedication to take charge of your life. You can be all you desire. The confident image and experience can be yours if you choose it.

# Discernment

**I**T IS IMPOSSIBLE to make appropriate choices and run your life optimally without listening to the voice of *discernment*. Discernment is that fine line in decision making that reveals the truth. Whenever your discernment is accurate and on target, you feel perfectly aligned, and your life flows smoothly. The challenge is to know whether you are operating from your higher power or the perspective of your ego.

When ego is in control, temptation and desire can be intense. You may feel a certain sensation or receive a strong impulse to do something. The attraction may be so strong that it is overwhelming and you react to it unconsciously. Because desire takes over, you may feel driven or falsely perceive that surrendering to the desire is your only direction. You may feel out of control or experience lack of balance in the process if you fail to consider that there is an alternate choice or if you go unconsciously on automatic to carry out your inclination.

An example of this might be the temptation to eat something you might normally consider to be out of order or inappropriate for the good or health of your body. When the desire hits, however, all resolutions and best intentions fly to the wind. You do not go through the conscious process of discriminating between the benefits and disadvantages of eating the particular food. Frequently you may bypass all conscious or mental processes for instant gratification. The desire is acted upon without "discernment," in other words. What is unfortunate about taking action without discernment is that sooner or later you suffer regret or remorse at the action you have taken. If you eat or drink not in accordance with your bodily needs, you may pay the price through undesirable results to the physical body or through the emotional imbalance of guilt. Extreme imbalance can be costly in "recovery time."

What would be involved in appropriate discernment concerning desires and temptations?

- The first step, naturally, is being aware of the desire.

- Next, put your impulsive action on hold for a moment to understand what is transpiring—that there is a possibility of your acting out of control which could result in unwanted consequences.

- Realize that you have a choice between at least two courses of action—to act immediately or to view the situation from a more enlightened perspective.

- Detach from the present moment, and project yourself into the future. Sense how you would feel first of all as a result of immediately following your initial impulse or temptation and secondly as a result of taking a more conservative course of action or perhaps refraining from any action. Which feels better down the road?

- Make your decision from the advantage point of expanded awareness.

You are incorporating a higher and greater consciousness by observing from a detached viewpoint prior to decision making. This process frees you from the imbalance and pain of guilt, regret, and remorse.

Discernment is necessary as an evolutionary step in consciousness until you arrive at the connection with your Higher Power which assists you to always make the appropriate decisions automatically. All areas of your life that involve learning through decision making and self-control are affected. In the early learning process, temptations occur in order to provide the opportunity to master discernment. You need to learn discernment in caring for the physical body, as discussed. Thoughts and emotions must be observed and controlled as well. Your financial, relationship, and career decisions are all a part of mastering discernment.

Why is it so challenging to make appropriate choices and decisions through discernment as well as to take control and responsibility for your life? A previous habit of responding unconsciously may have been established. The saving grace is that once you are aware of your temptations and make suitable changes, the old habits can be broken. You must, however, take charge and discern in order to be successful. There is no judgment here, and you are responsible for creating your own timetable for learning.

What are the benefits to mastering the concept of discernment other than increased balance, control, and growth? One of the major advantages is *freedom*. The old temptation has lost its power over you, and you act responsibly. Much time and energy are preserved when you are free from the inevitable regret, guilt, and remorse which serves to throw you even more out of balance. You acquire increased time and energy to spend in more productive ways. More and more opportunities open up to you when you have removed the old blockages from your energy field. The Universe recognizes your acceleration in "going beyond" what has held you back in the past and rewards you. You feel a lightness in this new freedom which carries over into all areas of your life. Freedom also leads to bliss.

The choice is yours, and the timetable is also up to you. All are freewill choices. The natural progression of integration and incorporation of discernment into your life is to finally "go on automatic," but *this time* on an elevated positive level and linked to your Higher Guiding Power. Temptation does not exist at this level because you have mastered it and gone to a higher state of being. You now have an innate sensing process to guide you away from negativity. It was always there—merely covered up in the past. It is your choice to experience the freedom and bliss of growth through discernment to higher levels of existence. The opportunity is *always* present.

# Freedom for Life

**T**HE ULTIMATE GOAL for millions of people throughout the world is freedom. In an increasing number of countries in which personal, social, and economic freedom has been restricted and is now being released, new opportunities appear. Freedom of movement is now affecting all areas of life. There has long been a separation between the "free world" and that part ruled by oppression and domination. As mass consciousness escalates, the oppression lifts and gives way to freedom. External freedom is a welcome improvement for most, although adjustments to a new way of being in the world must occur.

On another level, for every living being, the concept of individual internal freedom exists. This inner freedom is not dictated by others but by you and your state of mind. What does it really mean to be free? So many individuals dwell in prisons created by the mind. The only person who can truly free you is **YOU**.

What is involved in the lack of personal freedom conceived by the mind? One of the hindrances many people experience is self-limitation. The mind creates entire scenarios concerning what you can or cannot do. It places restrictions upon your abilities to accomplish things, go where you desire, and have all you want in life. You may feel trapped by life's circumstances and not be able to foresee your way out of challenges. The number of areas in which you can mentally imprison or limit yourself is endless.

Observe what your belief is that limits your sense of freedom. Do you feel worthy of what you want to do, be, and have? Are you critical of yourself, or do you consider others to be more deserving or competent? What is your consciousness about freedom? If you were "given" freedom in all areas of your life, what would be different?

In the "free world," people are so accustomed to placing restrictions and limitations upon themselves that they attempt to project them onto others as well. This occurs in governments, churches, legal systems, schools, and in almost every organization including marriage and family. A multitude of laws, rules, and regulations have been created which limit individual freedom in the guise of protection. It is not considered appropriate to "do as you please" much of the time. Creating laws to regulate and restrict others constitutes a full-time job for many individuals.

Now let us return to the restrictions you place on yourself through your own will. You and you alone can remove them. How do you respond to the demands, commands, and whims of others? Do you give yourself permission to attend to your own needs and desires? Do you allow yourself to look at what in your life requires change and then do you change it?

What is foremost is to observe your life as it truly is, **FREE OF JUDGMENT**. Ask yourself what is out of order or what appears to be holding you back. If your answer involves restrictions you have allowed others to impose upon you in any way, it may be in your best interest to express your feeling to those individuals. At the very least, be honest with yourself. The expression alone will serve to set you free, and infringements of the other individuals may have occurred without their conscious intent. Many people have control issues, and rather than concentrating on controlling themselves, they unconsciously attempt to control others.

If the restrictions holding you back are self-imposed, it is essential to pay close attention and take stock of how you are sabotaging your life and freedom. You might want to take the responsibility of freeing yourself from you—from your lack of self-confidence, guilt, unworthy feelings, fear, insecurity, and all negative thoughts and feelings. Wipe the slate clean in order to free yourself by releasing all that is no longer appropriate. It is not in order to continue on a path that you now find does not work for you. Set yourself free! Give yourself permission to change and be, do, and have what you desire. If you free yourself first, you will no longer attract others into your life who will attempt to restrict you because they will be unsuccessful when you have reclaimed control.

The more you work on securing your own personal freedom by giving yourself permission to be free—to live in your truth and not in sacrifice to others, the entire world benefits as well. The energy of freedom is contagious as you provide a role model for others. Remember, freedom begins in the mind and is demonstrated in your emotions and resulting life situations. Alter your mind to set yourself free. As always, ultimately the choice is yours.

# Choice for Life

**T**HE CONCEPT OF CHOICE has been intertwined throughout the preceding pages. It is now time to clarify and expand upon its importance in weaving your life's tapestry. Every day you have many, many choices to make—some major and some minor. We have talked about freewill choice, the freedom of choosing, and the responsibility of *choosing appropriately*.

What you must comprehend is that the choice in every matter is truly yours and therefore your responsibility. You would do well to release the mistaken notions that "others do it to you" and that you are a "victim of circumstances." When you observe clearly and objectively with a high degree of awareness, you will know that in each and every instance of your life, you exercise choice. It is impossible to avoid choosing. In allowing others to make decisions for you and your life, you are still "choosing to let them do so." If you feel manipulated or controlled by others, realize that you have made the choice to allow it. When you take control of your life and assume full responsibility for it, you have made that choice as well.

From the moment you awaken in the morning, you make the choices of whether or not to get out of bed, brush your teeth, and eat breakfast. You select what to eat and wear, who to communicate with, what to do in your free time, how to conduct your business, and many other options. There are also major life decisions involving relationships, careers, and paths of learning and growth.

The reason you may not be aware of the tremendous volume and vastness of choices presented to you and made by you each day is that many of them occur automatically at the subconscious level and may not even enter the arena of your thought process. Every time you drive a car, many choices are instinctively made such as when to accelerate, how much to brake, and when to begin turning the wheel. None of these activities requires much careful, time-consuming thought. They just spontaneously occur as a result of choices you made and learned from in the past and which you now accept as being the correct combination to "get you there safely." It would be very awkward and dangerous to take the time to consciously carry on an intricate step-by-step dialogue with yourself as to how to drive an automobile.

More than a few individuals choose to unconsciously float through life, following the path of least resistance. Others consciously challenge every aspect they encounter. For some, choice is easy and carried out with confidence. For others it signifies a struggle. The essential thing to realize is that you always do have choice, and with it comes the decision-making process along with assuming responsibility for the outcome. If you are dissatisfied with the situations in your life, acknowledge that they are the direct outcome of choices you have made in the past. Therefore, you may want to pay close attention to the choices you *now* make. Awareness is essential. Be conscious and mindful of what you choose to think, state, and feel on the more subtle inner level. The external, more obvious physical choices and decisions often present themselves as being more dominant and command a great deal of your attention. The decisions, for example, of where to live and work may consume many weeks or months of planning. Creating your environment is a continuous conscious process of making choices.

The more subtle, inner dimension decisions concerning what to think, feel, and express, however, comprise one of the greatest creative forces in your life. They are designed solely by you. You control the selection of what to think at every moment. *Thoughts* may enter your mind of their own accord, but it is your choice of what to do with those thoughts that is significant. You may accept them as truth or reject, alter, purify, reframe, ignore, or deny them. The same process occurs with feelings in a slightly different way. You can express, repress, control, or allow your emotions to be totally out of control. You may either be spontaneous or inhibited. You may knowingly choose what you want to think or feel if you are aware that you have the power to control your life by doing so. Conscious choice is how you create your life and circumstances.

At each moment you are free to choose joy or sadness, acceptance or resentment, love or fear. An emotion may arise for you, but it is your decision whether or not to accept it. If you feel anger, you can choose to retain this feeling for a moment, a lifetime, or anywhere in between. You can also choose to recognize that it exists, express it (or not express it), or release it and substitute acceptance, understanding, and love. The curious thing is that a choice must *always* be made because you cannot simultaneously retain two opposing emotions. Since you are continually required to make choices, you are constantly choosing between the positive and negative, balance and imbalance. Ultimately the choice is between love and fear. All negative emotions are incorporated into fear, and all positive emotions are wrapped up in love. Whenever you feel a negative emotion, you can dispel it by making the statement, "I choose love." You will feel a great energy shift by doing so.

When a greater number of your choices become positive than negative, your life changes dramatically, and a new pattern is created. Positive people and experiences are magnetically attracted to you as a result. The reverse is true as well with negative choices.

It is obvious, by now, the power and influence that are generated by your thought and feeling choices which occur on the more subtle inner level. Increased strength of creative choice is determined by the words you speak audibly and the emotions and actions you demonstrate. Every word carries with it a vibration to pull to you what you express, so you might consider choosing your words wisely. What you intend and verbalize is what you create. The stronger your intentions and feelings about what you state, the quicker the manifestation. This powerful concept is ever present for you to integrate into your life.

At all times you need to be aware that other people and situations have only the power and influence over you that you *choose* to give them. Consciously or unconsciously, **YOU ARE IN CONTROL**. It is up to you to exercise your gift of choice at the *conscious* level. If you choose to live and operate unconsciously, choices are still made but often carry with them undesirable effects. The decision is yours whether or not to assume conscious responsibility. Whatever you choose is perfect for your learning.

# Persistence for Life

**D**ETERMINATION AND dedication of purpose can only be realized and produce successful results through an attitude of persistence. All the noble intentions and goal setting in the world are futile if they are not carried through to completion.

Clarity of purpose needs to be kept foremost in the mind at all times, and the desire for successful fulfillment must be sustained. The energy of determination or "never giving up" is an essential ingredient in achieving and fulfilling goals. Those who truly believe in their objectives have a head start because they begin with a sense of dedication. If you strongly *intend* to accomplish what you begin, you are more likely to persist until you achieve successful completion.

Two individuals with identical goals and original intent may experience entirely different results. The reason is that one person's dedication leads to a higher level or degree of persistence.

How does the concept of persistence affect your everyday life? Any project or action you undertake is affected by your dedication, determination, and resulting tenaciousness. "Giving up" is the opposite condition which only serves to hold you back. This does *not*, however, mean that it is fitting for you to persevere in a goal if you honestly have a shift of purpose. Discernment is always in order to ascertain the appropriateness of your goal and the pursuit of it. It may be useful to frequently observe how you are progressing toward your goals and to honestly determine if the present path still feels like the correct one for you. Persistence is a necessary ingredient when all is in order and on course. If your intent, truth, or purpose changes, all the persistence you can muster will not result in successful completion.

Persistence can occur only when a high level of dedication is present. When it is, persistence becomes a valuable catalyst. It paves the way to success through untold obstacles. Although it most often serves to be your greatest ally, it can also prove to be a challenging adversary. If you persist in an endeavor that no longer is inappropriate, or perhaps never was, you might throw yourself out of balance. Stubborn persistence towards an objective that is out of order is like bumping your head against a brick wall. It is OK to change your mind and direction at any given moment in pursuing your truth. Shifts of energy occur spontaneously as do changes in the individuals and situations surrounding you. If a course of action suddenly feels wrong, out of balance, or uncomfortable, stop immediately! Search out and investigate the situation. Listen to what your inner voice is communicating to you. Chances are that if the direction of your path is to change, you will quickly become aware. Persisting on an old inappropriate path out of stubbornness only results in frustration and failure. This is false persistence. Once you develop your conscious awareness, you will know immediately which avenues to pursue.

Persistence, then, is valuable only when the goal is still worth pursuing. When it is, persistence often provides the necessary component for success. Why is persisting so challenging, and why do you "give up" before achieving what you determine to be your appropriate goals, desires, and dreams? Your dedication and determination may originally have been present, and then something happens. You do not "feel" like continuing. You may be distracted by other projects or issues. You make up excuses or delays and procrastinate.

What is really occurring? This is one of the greatest stumbling blocks of mankind and is responsible for most unachieved dreams and goals. It is called **SELF-SABOTAGE**. Self-sabotage can rear its ugly head at any moment and can creep into your life to jeopardize and destroy your dreams and desires. Self-sabotage does not enter from the external world. It is created from within.

The most common form of self-sabotage occurs out of a feeling of unworthiness or guilt. If you do not feel deep within your being that you deserve your goal or dream, you will find a way to sabotage its fulfillment. The most characteristic technique used and "created by you" is procrastination. Persistence falls by the wayside so that you can achieve your self-fulfilling belief of unworthiness.

To avoid this situation, the first step after formulating your dreams, desires, and goals is to sense whether or not you can actually comfortably see and feel yourself living in the new desired role or reality. Is there a twinge of guilt or a slightly uncomfortable feeling that you do not deserve it? Put yourself into the space of having successfully completed your goal and honestly observe if it feels compatible with who you are. If it does, wonderful! Persistence will work powerfully for you. If any doubt or discomfort exists, you may need to work on inner worthiness issues and increase your level of self-esteem.

Once you feel comfortable concerning your desired role or pursuit, observe your level of excitement or passion surrounding it. You must possess the emotional "charge" in order to retain a high level of persistence. Passion or emotion is the power and guiding force behind persistence. Without it, you are merely "plodding along" rather than "being driven." Persistence is sustained through daily repetition, reinforcement, and rededication.

All must work together in harmony—first the goal, comfort level, and finally the passion must be strongly present. With all in place, "balanced persistence" is the key. "Balance" is symbolized by the ordering and structuring of your life in such a way that you do not lose sight of the other factors essential to your health and well-being. Healthful persistence of a goal includes proper rest and nourishment on all levels—physical, mental, emotional, and spiritual. If all is thrown to the wind in the heat of passion toward a goal, imbalances and illness can occur. Take time each day to engage in a balanced apportionment of physical, mental, emotional, and spiritual activities to maintain wholeness and completeness as a person. This further increases your potential and energy level. All things being present in balance and order, persistence is the connecting link to successfully bring you to your goal. Without it, all good intentions fall by the wayside.

The speed with which you achieve your goals is not important. You may encounter obstacles or detours. These are merely opportunities for further learning and present themselves as tests or challenges of your dedication and commitment. What is of essence is how you interchange with the obstacles. Do you allow them to throw you off course (self-sabotage)? Or do you observe them as positive challenges to resolve and grow from? Do you give up or do you persevere?

As always, the choice is yours. Through persistence, you have the potential joy of receiving one of life's greatest rewards—satisfaction. Once you experience fulfillment, you will feel reawakened with greater inspiration toward achieving even higher levels and goals. The choice is basically between balanced, appropriate persistence which catapults you forward in life and self-sabotage which holds you back. You will most likely have the opportunity during your life to experience and learn from both.

# Discipline for Life

**E**XHIBITING THE NECESSARY self-discipline to achieve your goals often presents a major challenge. On a daily basis it may be tempting to procrastinate because negative mind energy intrudes and creates various obstacles to your doing what you feel you must do. Commitment wavers and soon guilt enters in.

You may have been reared with the idea that discipline means struggle, challenge, and having to do something other than what you would rather be doing. It might mean performing a task or routine at a precise time each day or denying yourself what you want to do in favor of something you consider more uplifting or appropriate. You may restrict or circumvent yourself from having what you desire.

Whatever your concept of discipline, it most likely involves or implies hardship, contest, or something contrary to your present wishes, desires, or preferences. This is in reality, a mistaken notion. The more appropriate perception and practice of self-discipline is to tune in on a constant basis to what you are inwardly feeling, hearing, and experiencing. You are being perfectly guided at every moment by the Power Within. What you might have thought was positive self-discipline in the past may be contrary to what is appropriate at present. Planning your schedule or routine or creating your resolutions may originally have felt right. In actuality, it may have been appropriate for the moment, not necessarily forever. What is fitting now is what your inner guidance is communicating to you, and it is perfectly acceptable if that is different from what you originally designed. What is essential is to be aware in the present and to do what feels most suitable for you now. Surrender to your inner Guidance. You may have to ignore the chiding or criticism of others and your initial feelings of guilt when you first begin to "change the rules" until you become comfortable with "living your truth." It is totally in order for you to change your mind or course of action (or alter the rules) because circumstances change and energy shifts.

One area of caution is to be sure to use "discernment" to determine if you are changing the rules out of appropriateness or as a result of laziness or temptation. Honesty with yourself is necessary to determine your true feelings.

Certain areas of discipline, then, are appropriate only as long as they are useful. Attempting to force dedication or commitment to a project, ideal, or goal past its level of working for you only serves to throw you off balance. An obvious challenge arises when others are involved in a group effort and strict guidelines have been created. You may want to consider, prior to "signing up," if you choose to be at the mercy of someone else's decisions which determine and often restrict *your* life's scheduling and your own decisions. If you allow yourself to become involved in other's group reality, there is danger of losing control of your own true self and self-determination. You may benefit from "feeling out" the potential hazards of group reality before joining. Do you choose to discipline yourself to another's judgment or belief system, or do you wish to remain in integrity with yourself?

If you make the choice to live and act in integrity with yourself, the concept of self-discipline transforms into one of living in your truth and self-determination. You are marching to the beat of your own drummer rather than following the herd. The only valid self-discipline is to be true to yourself.

This initially can be a challenging course of action or way of "being" in the world because it requires strength of character to be unaffected by the resulting possible judgments and criticisms from others who love to imagine and suggest exactly what you "should" be doing and when. You may need all the courage you can gather to depart from the expectations and manipulations of others when you first commit to your true "self-discipline." Commitment to be your own person is a step in personal growth and self-validation. It requires the decision to ignore what used to guide your life from the external world and to recover your strength and power from within. Others lose power over you which was a power they did not rightfully own. You gave it to them before you realized the power and completeness within yourself. You have all your answers. You and you alone know what is in order for you at any particular time. Be aware of the imbalance you feel when you surrender your will to another's desires and opinions. You may want to consider disciplining yourself to the ultimate goal—to be true to yourself. Of course, aligned with this decision is a commitment or promise that you not interfere with others' self-determination or judge, evaluate, or be involved with deciding what is appropriate for those around you. If you feel that others lack self-discipline, you may be seeing a reflection of yourself. When you have disciplined yourself and released enough negative impulses, you will be totally unaffected by the activities and judgments of other people.

The correct discipline to be involved in is balancing and organizing your life according to what is true for you at present. Since it is important to remain flexible and open to change, resist the temptation to force and retain a previous decision or determination if it no longer works for you. This is not discipline. It is stubborn unconsciousness. Live consciously in the present in order to control your life.

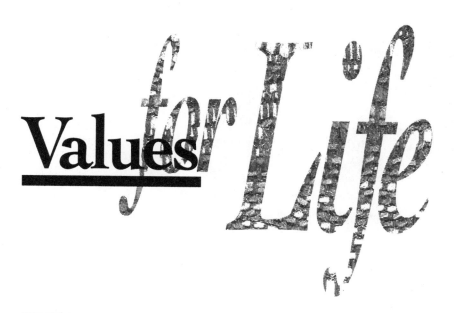

# Values for Life

**FROM THE MOMENT** of your birth, you inherit the value system of your family or caretakers and the structures of society. During the early formative years, you adopt values through interaction with other individuals. You learn respect and reverence for certain concepts, philosophies, and beliefs. An evaluative or judgment system is unconsciously created. In the beginning, all you observe and accept is colored or influenced by the value systems of others.

Eventually you become aware that there is a difference between what you inwardly "hold to be dear" and the analytical and judgmental belief systems and manipulations from outside. You may develop inner values that are in opposition to those widely held by friends, family, neighbors, and acquaintances, and yet you may be in agreement on others. Your own particular unique blend of values contributes to your individuality.

What is important now is to look at and review objectively the values you have accepted because quite often they unconsciously have crept into your consciousness through "osmosis" and without individual contemplation. If your father worshipped money, do you accept the value he placed upon money as your own? Do you question the appropriateness of actions or beliefs for yourself personally? What value do you place on material possessions? Have you ever thought about it, or do you accept, as your own, the value placed on them by others? There is no "right" or "wrong." The important thing is to independently establish your own value system.

Every day you make value assessments on people, experiences, and a wide range of options. Since your value system is the determining factor in your decision making, it pays to be aware. It is important to be in integrity with your own value system rather than blindly accepting that of another. The approach must, however, be done not only with your own best interests in mind but also free of judging or evaluating the correctness of other's values for themselves. Detach from "judging" values. What is of value to one person may not be for anyone else, but that does not diminish the significance to that person. Remember, you cannot understand the paths of others unless you achieve the nearly impossible task of walking in their shoes.

Your outer values are easily recognized by the external choices and decisions you make. You choose your living conditions and life style. Nutritional choices include a diet of junk food or healthy, live food. You select your career according to how you have educated or prepared yourself. Life partners are chosen according to what you personally value. Friends, opportunities, activities, and all experiences are either elected or rejected relative to values you have accepted externally and internally.

What may be less easily recognized by others is your inner or internal value system which you may not share openly on a conscious level. It may even dwell in your unconscious and without your full understanding. Earlier it was stated that certain values are unconsciously accepted by you merely by the fact of your being born into a family which honors or supports those values. Now these inherited values can serve you well as a learning process when you take the responsibility to consider them as being outside yourself. Detach from them in order to observe if they assist you in a positive way at this time. Are they comfortable and do they "feel" appropriate, or is there some uncertainty? It is time to sort through your values and beliefs and ask, one-by-one, "Is this of value to me now? Am I in integrity with myself or have I blindly or unconsciously accepted the values of others without question or discernment?"

If you resist observing your way of "being" in the world as a result of your unique blend of values, you cannot have true self-understanding. You may lose sight of where other people and their values end and you begin. Boundaries become foggy as you lose your self-clarity.

All values and value systems serve their purpose on many levels. They all exist for growth and learning. You move in life from judgment to acceptance, from unconsciousness to responsible consciousness. Your progression through life is determined by your own inner strength and integrity. How much or how long will you choose to be guided under the influence of others? When will you move into the strength, conviction, and determination of your own inner guidance which is your truth?

Your value system is functioning "in order" or "in balance" when you feel free of resistance and guilt and are confident of the way you choose to run your life. You are not swayed by the criticisms or "helpful" suggestions by well-meaning individuals. You know you are free when you are able to observe and reject the old parental values you were reared with that now are inappropriate for you. When all is operating well within your value system, you are also free from concern over what others may think. It is safe for you to have values separate from those of mainstream society, and you feel no need to justify or validate them to anyone.

You are healthy when you are comfortable with the choices and decisions you make guided from within—free of external or inherited influences. First you must be able to separate and discern which values originated with you and which evolved from another. If they came from someone else and are accepted by you, are they still appropriate?

Values, then, are in a constant state of flux and may change according to your maturation and illumination. They may be accepted and adapted or rejected at any time. There is no need to rigidly or stubbornly retain old values no matter how good or honorable they once "appeared" if they lack importance or credibility now.

Allow yourself the freeing experience to reorganize your own personal value system. You may have some pleasant surprises in store as you find yourself feeling lighter and freer and more in control of your life.

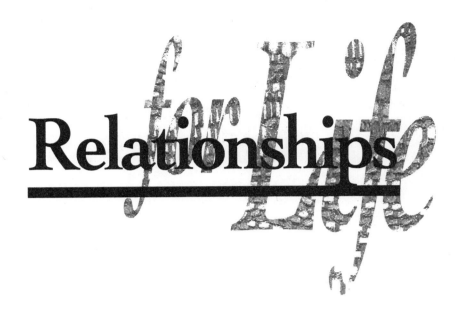

# Relationships

**RELATIONSHIPS CAN** constitute the most rewarding and yet challenging learning experiences because they constantly surround you with both opportunities and frustrations. Connections with others are inescapable unless you choose a life of seclusion. However, since most choose to be a part of this world and participate in the framework of interaction with others, relationships become an important focus.

As a child you quickly learn that everyone is *not* exactly like you. Each has his or her own unique personality and way of being in the world. There are those who are fun to be around and those you want to avoid, but all have their own special value in relation to you. Each and every relationship is formed to teach you something about life, the world, and especially yourself. You can experience a great adventure in self-discovery merely by studying the relationships in your life that surround and challenge you because, at some level, they are an energy reflection of you. Each individual in your life represents a part of you that you may be unaware of at present. You learn self-acceptance by accepting others.

By looking at and recognizing certain significant characteristics in others, you are acknowledging them in yourself. It would be difficult to recognize these aspects if they were not a part of you or your consciousness. This may sound shocking, and your first impulse might be to negate or deny this statement. To shed some light on this matter, let us look at the way energy operates. In the Universe, physical opposites attract and bring polar balance and harmony. Spiritually, "like" energies of kindred souls are magnetized together to promote balance and harmony. Various energies co-exist in perfect order for a purpose. You definitely *do notice* and are often shaken into instant awareness by certain characteristics of others with whom you are in a relationship. They might seem so bizarre or foreign that it seems impossible they could in any way be related to you. Rather than perceiving them as they initially appear, often a little creative observation is required because the "form" might be different. You might need to generalize the noticeable aspects or broaden their scope before you can recognize them as a part of you.

✗ The preferred way to accomplish this process is to ask your inner self to assist you to learn what it is about yourself that you can discover from the relationships in your life. For greater understanding and clarity, take one relationship at a time. Close your eyes and ask, "How am I like so and so? How do I demonstrate his or her characteristics?"

✗ You may find some surprising first impressions and astonishing answers if you are open minded and honest with yourself.

✗ If nothing initially comes to mind, employ the technique of detachment. Step aside in your mind's eye and observe yourself and the other individual as though you were totally unrelated to each other. It is easier to see the similarities when you are free of encompassing emotions.

✗ Once you uncover the resemblance, you achieve a heightened sense of self-awareness.

✗ Acknowledge yourself for the honesty, strength, and courage this process takes because at first you may feel vulnerable, unmasked, or exposed, particularly if that characteristic you see in another and reflected by you is one you would rather not possess.

✿ Once you are aware of the attribute, you can decide whether you wish to retain or release that part of you, or perhaps modify or reframe it in some manner.

So far, the content of this message is that the negativity you observe in others is a reflection of a part of yourself that you have suppressed or denied or are merely unaware of at present. This process works in reverse as well. If there are characteristics of the individuals in your life that you love, admire, respect, and even envy, know that these desirable aspects are a reflection of you as well. You may not be aware of them if you are accustomed to examining yourself with a critical eye, but they exist nonetheless. Accept and claim them as a wonderful new discovery as more of your total person becomes revealed to you.

It has been illustrated how relationships teach you about yourself and broaden your self-concept and awareness. Relationships can also challenge your ability to stay centered, balanced, and focused on your path and self-integrity. The challenge appears in diversion, distraction, and disruption from remaining centered and balanced in your truth. You may have your day perfectly arranged exactly as you desire it to be when unexpectedly someone enters your life with an issue or demand that threatens to change all your plans. You are forced to make a decision whether or not to alter your day (and life) according to the requests of another. There is danger of being thrown off guard and out of balance in a situation in which one part of you wants to continue in your initial original direction and another part of you wants to assist by altering your course due to the unforeseen interaction with someone in your life. Although you might feel some discomfort or frustration at this point, realize that this is occurring as a lesson and opportunity to learn to make the choice to live at your highest level of truth—to make the decisions which will keep you in balance and in integrity with yourself. It is highly recommended that you remember you have an option and responsibility to say "no" to another if what they desire is not in your own best interest. Realize that the roles of others represent "teachers" for you. That is what is important to be conscious of rather than the individual emotion of the issue or diversion.

- At this point, you need to recognize the value of remaining conscious, centered, and focused in the present moment.

- Reject any past unconscious pattern of responding to individuals.

- Feel the emotions you are experiencing at a deep inner level and ask for their meaning to be revealed to you.

- Give yourself permission to respond to another's needs and desires compassionately but in balance with your own. You must first act out of truth and integrity with yourself.

- If the other individuals are angry or resentful and react negatively to your decisions, keep your centered focus and remember that your role is also to be a "teacher" for them. This gives them an opportunity to learn from their own reactions and feelings in relation to you.

Although challenging, relationships are your greatest gifts. When you understand that they are created and attracted to you out of love, it is easier to accept the opportunity to learn from them. Treasure your relationships with gratitude as they teach you that all is interconnected as a beautifully orchestrated tapestry of life. All thoughts, feelings, and actions interact with those of others as you become both teacher and student.

# Habits for Life

**I**T IS CUSTOMARY throughout the course of life to develop regular ways of doing routine things and responding to similar situations. A habit is formed and ingrained when thought is separated from behavior. The behavior occurs more or less automatically, frequently, and consistently. There is a level of mind that accepts and perpetuates the habit without thinking about it.

To change or alter a habit, a conscious intent is usually required. It is also a challenge to "break" a habit because the central nervous system is linked with the subconscious, and both have an intrinsic agreement to continue the habit unless reprogrammed.

There are multitudes of things we do daily in nearly identical patterns because we are creatures of habit. To terminate or transform a habit, often a very strong desire is required, especially if the habit involves addictions.

First, it must be stated that many habits are beneficial, and it is important to reinforce these. It is positive to maintain the habits of greeting people with a beautiful smile, of being kind, or remaining organized. Generally, however, the connotation of "habit" usually involves a desire for positive change.

The concept or notion of habits opens up an entire realm for self-discovery and understanding. Why do you react or respond in a certain way? Why do you unconsciously reach for a cigarette when you already have one lit and resting in your ashtray? Why do you park in the same parking spot every day or eat dinner each evening at 6:00 P.M.? Most habits generate a feeling of comfort because they represent familiarity. Because habits are a "known," they impart an aura of well-being even though that may be inaccurate in reality.

The appropriateness of habits may involve the degree or intensity you are attached to them. In situations of great magnitude, the habit can become an addiction. Tobacco, alcohol, and drugs might come to mind, but addictions can involve anything at all if you give them the power to interfere with or interrupt the perfect balance in your life. If it is not beneficial, you might conclude that you would be better off to be free of your habit or addiction.

When you make the decision to terminate your habit or addiction, you must be sincere, dedicated, and determined at a deep inner level to be successful. A half-hearted effort rarely succeeds. You might wish to end certain habits and retain others. The important thing is that you must be committed and "ready" to make the change which cannot occur before you genuinely desire it. The redirection must also be *your* personal decision rather than the result of wishes or demands from others. Commitment must be present.

⚜ Acknowledge, without judging yourself, that you have a habit. Is it useful or is it inconvenient, harmful, or annoying?

⚜ You may need to detach and view the process from a distance to understand what is desirable or undesirable and why.

⚜ Allow yourself an honest, non-judgmental decision whether or not to end the habit at this time. (It may be serving you in some way that would cause disruption if you commit to change before you are ready.) All is accomplished at the appropriate time.

ᚦ What may be helpful is a dramatic, enlightened, and often emotional shift of consciousness. You may suddenly feel disgust and repulsion from the old habit. This significantly heightens your dedication for change.

ᚦ When your commitment is intact, what is your best course of action? Look within for your own personal guidance at this point. For some, gradual change is in order. For others, immediate (cold turkey) transformation is appropriate. For all, deep concentration on the desired way of being with *no* thought to the undesired behavior is essential.

There is no single right or wrong method. All is undertaken and accomplished for your perfect learning and growth process. At some level you probably realize that negative habits and addictions hold you back. They may either cause only minor interference in your life or totally incapacitate or immobilize you. If you want to be aware of your life's challenges, they usually involve a process of you surmounting whatever is interfering with your life and keeping you from fulfillment and happiness. You cannot be truly happy and free if you feel out of control or are a slave to something contrary to what is best for you. If you procrastinate in overcoming a negative habit, be aware that the effects can and often do accelerate in an unfavorable way to create greater problems or obstacles for you until you learn all that you need to learn from the experiences.

Although there are various external means of assisting you to overcome habits and addictions, the commitment must be internal in order to release the self-sabotage which is usually involved. Once again, detach from yourself and emotions to observe clearly what is occurring within you. To achieve greater clarity and honesty, approach it from the point of view that it is another person's problem or issue.

It may be useful to know that often habits are created in order to provide something for you or to protect you from something. In some cases they serve as punishment for those who consciously or unconsciously desire to be punished. Look carefully at what they provide for you—short term and long term—positive or negative.

Your level of comprehension must increase in order to move forward in life. The habit of negative thinking is a major issue for many people to overcome. It is your freewill choice whether or not to deal with your negative habits. You may choose to release them, alter them, or presently deny them. Whatever you choose is for your growth and learning. Habits and addictions represent tools to assist you in your self-discovery. Open your heart to see more clearly.

# Completion *for Life*

**D**O YOU EVER FIND yourself feeling unfulfilled or that something is missing or unfinished? If so, what that means is that you are lacking completion within a certain aspect of your life. It can involve relationships, careers, finances or any other issue. It is unfinished business.

Unfinished business is one of the greatest energy blocks known to mankind. The full circle of energy completion has not connected in an appropriate manner. The incomplete part is *out there somewhere* or *inside of you* begging for attention, satisfaction, or conclusion.

If you have nagging thoughts or unsettled feelings about the past, you also have unfinished business. Have you ended a relationship with someone a while ago and still have difficulty when you see that person? Do you think of that person or relationship a large portion of the time or feel an emotional charge at the mention of the person's name? This means that you are not complete with the relationship. Have you ever been involved in a situation or activity which you withdrew from without explanation and then felt guilty about what you considered to be "letting people down?" Have you pursued an area of education or career that was never finished and, as a result, do you wonder what you would be doing differently if you had completed the training?

It is the unknown and uncertainty, or feeling of lack of fulfillment and completion, that can be troublesome in all these cases or situations. People can become stuck in their lives without realizing that old unfinished business is what is holding them back. How do you find the stagnating causes and heal this in yourself?

- Sit quietly and clear your mind.

- Imagine a large movie screen before you and ask your subconscious to reveal to you the most important thing in your life that is incomplete. It may help to close your eyes.

- Let the picture or recollection develop before you. You may actually see images in your mind's eye if you are visual. You may simply remember a situation or receive a subtle impression of what is incomplete.

- When you have obtained the information, you have options. You can do nothing and retain the blockage, or you can complete the process. You will need to shift the energy in one way or another. There are a variety of techniques that can assist you.

- If your unfinished business involves a person that you need to release or communicate with, you can visit or call the person on the phone and express what you feel you need to say to achieve completion. If you are not comfortable doing this, or if the person has disappeared or passed on, you can write a letter containing all you wish to tell that person. It is the very act of writing that can finalize the situation, and writing is one of the most powerful tools available to you. It is not necessary to mail the letter. Often it is preferable to burn it as a symbol of the purification of completion.

❦ Another technique is to sit quietly and bring the relationship or situation that is incomplete into your mind's eye. Change the sequence of events in your mind, and imagine yourself doing or saying what is appropriate to tie up the loose ends. Strongly imagine all to be exactly as you desire. You will feel the energy shift.

You may create original methods of completion that are unique to you and your situation. The important thing is to do it. Examine *all* areas of your life that are incomplete and resolve them in your own way. Perhaps you will rekindle a former area of interest or study in which you were once involved such as a sport, musical instrument, or hobby that you once enjoyed and now miss. Involve yourself with unfinished projects around the house that are causing blockages. Reorganize and clear out everything in your life that is no longer useful. Pursue your dream of travel or advanced education. What is important is to become clear on what is holding you back in your life. Then decide what to do about it. You can remain stuck, or you can go beyond by completion. Your possibilities and potential in life are limitless once you release the obstacles and complete what needs to be done. You are then free and equipped to use your full amount of energy to move forward.

When you achieve completion in even one area of your life, you feel a significant change. Your personal satisfaction is tremendous and inspires you to address the other needy areas as well. You are aware of what needs to be done to feel fulfilled. Completion leads to wholeness of body, mind, and spirit. Uncluttered by unfinished business, you can take charge of your physical body and mental attitudes, achieve your full potential, and experience the lightness and freedom of spiritual growth that will set you free. It is impossible to achieve wholeness in your life if you have incomplete dangling particles. If you procrastinate and ignore or deny them, you place yourself in a mode of self-sabotage, becoming your own worst enemy by refusing to complete your life's processes. The choice as always is up to you.

All will be accomplished in time. It is up to you to make the choice to obtain fulfillment now through realization of all that was incomplete in the past or to continue the struggle with unfinished business.